THE
FIRST
40

THE FIRST 40

Brodee Reed

THE FIRST 40

iUniverse books may be ordered through booksellers or by contacting:

iUniverse
1663 Liberty Drive
Bloomington, IN 47403
www.iuniverse.com
1-800-Authors (1-800-288-4677)

Because of the dynamic nature of the Internet, any web addresses or links contained in this book may have changed since publication and may no longer be valid. The views expressed in this work are solely those of the author and do not necessarily reflect the views of the publisher, and the publisher hereby disclaims any responsibility for them.

Any people depicted in stock imagery provided by Getty Images are models, and such images are being used for illustrative purposes only. Certain stock imagery © Getty Images.

ISBN: 978-1-5320-7860-6 (sc)
ISBN: 978-1-5320-7861-3 (e)

Library of Congress Control Number: 2019910086

Print information available on the last page.

iUniverse rev. date: 07/18/2019

TOSSING DEMONS

"Brodee! Brodee! Are you okay?"

Confused I raised my head, it took a few minutes to realize where I was. Wearing only shorts, a shirt and flip flops, even though it was freezing outside, I exhaled and I could see my alcohol-soaked breath. I struggled to pull myself up, my body was sore, stiff and indented with ripples from the liner of my pick-up truck bed. I was a mess. The whole day I had been drowning myself in Bud Lite and Tequila shots, probably enough alcohol to get a German soccer team drunk.

This is where I was in my life. I would wake up, drive Lyft for the majority of the morning, then head to the gym around 1030 to sweat out the poison I put in my body from the day before. After a good sweat from lifting weights, a nice run/jog or brisk walk…oh who the hell am I kidding? After twenty minutes on the elliptical and drenched like a duck in a rain storm, I would shower, shit, shave and start making my rounds at the local bars. Yes, where everyone knew my name.

I had to finally ask myself, have I become an alcoholic? Have I lost all control of being a responsible father, husband, or adult? How much longer could my family, conscience and physical health take of my daily routine of drinking until I passed out or drank myself sober?

To answer all those questions, that was the last straw.

That night in the back of my truck hearing that sweet voice, Brodee, Brodee, are you okay? It was Sarah the bartender, and I was parked right in front of one of my favorite bars, the year was 2017.

1

My beautiful wife (MBW) and I had been fighting constantly prior to this day, she gave me an ultimatum. I stop drinking, or she was leaving. So, I said bye Felicia, HAHAHA, just kidding love.

That same evening before I ended up in the bed of my truck, I had to talk to my son, I had to apologize to him. Nothing would be right if I didn't have his love and support, I needed him.

My awesome son (MAS), lives with my ex-wife, I had asked her if I could visit with him. She agreed knowing I had been drinking all day, but I didn't drive with him anywhere. He came downstairs and sat in my truck. As soon as he looked at me tears started flowing down my face, he responded the same. This wasn't the first time I have had to leave him. I have also had to leave him due to several military deployments. I told him in short breaths, I was leaving the next day for a month. I told him how sorry I was for not being myself. We cried together for thirty minutes, and then at the end with tears drying up, I said, but when I get back, I am going to whoop yo ass at basketball, HAHAHA! He understood what I was going through, he gave me his support one hundred percent. He is a strong boy, full of heart. With his love and support, and my wife's love and caring heart I was determined to get help.

November 28th, 2017, MBW took me to the airport. It was a sobering drive. I was humble, motivated and ready to rid my head of the demons I have collected over the years. I needed help.

I was headed for a new beginning. Once my plane landed a green shirt lady was to be there to take me to the rehab center.

The first five days after my arrival I went through detox, they gave me these pills to help with the withdrawals and trust me. That shit worked. Following the detox process, I was ready to start the program. It consisted of classes varying from addiction, family, meditation, and basically ways to live a sober life. I embraced it all and was able to get to know myself again and figure out who I was. I learned to meditate. I used to laugh at people who would meditate, but in theory I wish I had done it my whole life, I wouldn't have been such a worry wort!

Every morning before breakfast I would walk around the compound. It had a pond with two turtles, I named them T1 and T2. There were two barracks, one for the females, our kitchen and day room, the other one was for the males. There was also two run-down tennis courts, a gym that looked like a parking garage, even a basketball and volleyball courts. It was home for a month. The food was great. I gained some weight, I but felt healthier due to the absence of alcohol.

On my morning walks my goal was ten thousand steps on my Fitbit. I smashed that goal every morning and each morning I would struggle to pull a demon out of my imaginary back pack and picture drowning that demon son of a bitch in the pond. By the end of my thirty days I would be demon free of all the bad stuff in my past.

My roommate was a great guy from the Pacific Northwest, he was a husband and a father. We got along great. I lucked out there! Who wants the snoring bastard that won't stop talking to you about Nascar and guns? Not me! We talked sports and women.

Although I was at an addiction center, my first forty is not all about drinking, drugs, rehab, and bad stuff that I did. It's all about my life as a father, Soldier, husband, seventies, eighties, and nineties kid. About great times, bad times with our country, and myself. About people around the world, traveling, vacations, presidents, athletes, music, movies, our great country. About confidence, anxiety, being a man, sports, and coaching. Yes, I ended up in rehab, but sometimes in life we as humans need to check ourselves! We need help to get back on track! To keep pushing forward! To heal! To forgive and try to forget!

It was day thirty, I was ready to head home, I was ready to start a new beginning. I met some great people at rehab, counselors, addicts and nurses, oh and the kitchen staff, they were amazing as well.

I landed back home on December 28th, 2017, just in time for the New Year. This new year was different, I was in bed by eight...sober. I woke up January 1st, 2018, clear headed, motivated and ready to kick the year off right. I felt clean.

Here I am! A new person with a different approach on life. I relied on my higher power to keep me anxiety free, humble and content with the past forty years.

My routine changed to AA meetings every morning at 630, which were great meetings, and a good way to start the day off! I will get into that later. I left there and immediately started picking passengers up driving Lyft. I would do this until around eleven in the morning, and then I would hit the gym for a much harder workout than before. I would do twenty five minutes on the elliptical, a nice massage chair for ten minutes, followed by walking a flight of stairs. Life was good! The rest of the day consisted of runs to the grocery store, chores, my house was spot less, and finishing the day with cooking my wife dinner. My roommate from rehab would text me on a daily basis, telling me how his day was going. We wouldn't talk sobriety between us, we always talked sports, and then something terrible happened.

January 24th, 2018, I received several texts, and looked at Facebook only to learn that he had passed away. He was to turn forty later that year. I didn't want to know, nor did I care what he had passed away from, he was gone! He struggled with a horrible disease called addiction. In a few brief texts from friends at the addiction center, his passing away was alcohol related. His death hit me hard, he was such a good guy, he shared pictures with me of when he was a rugby player, he was big, strong and healthy. One would think that it would never happen to a person of his stature. Addiction doesn't care. He loved his wife and step son, he was a car salesman, he was excited about a new job selling motorhomes, he was passionate about rugby, sports, he was tall, dark, and handsome. Best of all, he was a joy to be around. He wasn't a drunk, or drug addict, he was a man fighting a deadly disease.

R.I.P brother, thank you for being a part of my life.

Weeks before the passing of my roommate I began to write my book. This was the first time as far as I can remember that I was mentally stable and content with where I was in life. I have always wanted to write a book, and I tell myself, if nothing comes of it, at least I can say…I wrote a book.

January 11th, 2018 I began, it was easy to write. I have a lot to share. I learned I cannot just write anywhere, it needs to be the perfect place.

MBW has been wanting to go snowboarding for the longest time, so I tagged along with her. I knew going to the mountains would be a perfect place to write, and no doubt it was. Looking through a huge condo window at that beautiful mountainous resort, I see nothing but calm. Fresh mountain snow, tall healthy pine trees that surround winding ski slopes. Black birds posing on top of arched roof tops, and light poles. Buses move along smoothly through soft powder snow dropping off skiers and snowboarders, the American flag is slightly drifting through the crisp mountain air. I wrote for hours; my mind was clear.

Time passed and everything was still great. I loved writing, it gave me a sense of purpose in life. Then one day I felt like all my hard work was about to go out the window when my ex-wife came up with this out of the world freaking idea that she wanted to move to a different state on the other side of the country and take my son with her. Damn, I was pissed! I didn't know what to do! Do I tell my wife we need to move across the country? Do I take my ex-wife to court to try to keep my son in the state we live in now? Do I fly out to where they are moving twice a month? I didn't know! I ended up meditating a lot to stay calm and tell myself it is in God's hands, and everything will work out.

I had to tell my wife, her first response was fuck no, we are not moving across the country to the East coast. First of all Tom Brady lives in New England, and second of all its cold as balls. Yep, that was the response I got, and honestly the reaction I was expecting. I was stuck in between making my son happy and making my wife happy. Being the awesome wife she is, she came up with a plan for me to fly out to the East coast. She even said I could stay for a few weeks at a time, we would have the extra money because I would not have to pay child support due to my son living out of state. My son and I were content with that, it would all work out. Then out of nowhere my wife says she was ready to begin a new start somewhere else, and welcomed the idea of moving. I was pleased and it was such a relief. I wasn't pissed at the ex-wife anymore.

We flew to New England in early April, it was mud season, but I fell in love with it immediately. The ocean, rivers, trees, the abundance of lakes, they even have moose crossing signs. I love Moose. My anxiety was little to none, this was our new home.

A childhood friend I grew up with and have talked to on a weekly basis for twenty seven years, Henry, has lived in the New England area for six years. She and her husband have four beautiful girls and it just so happened when the wife and I were shopping for houses we found a great home two miles from Henry and her family. God was on our side.

We made an offer on the house, they accepted, we flew back home and began to plan our trip to move across the country. It was a big step for us, but we were determined. Everything fell into place, we found great renters to rent our townhome, MBW found an awesome job as a veterinary technician, she is a lover of animals. As far as me, I was going to continue to drive Lyft and write my story.

The day came to leave our current home for good, we had the Uhaul packed! So packed as I was pulling down the back door while simultaneously shoving socks, pens, keychains anything and everything small in size into the back. MBW followed me in our Kia with our four furry kids, Mili, Mini, Mighty, and Moose, four incredible cats. We were off, it took us a total of five days, we were in no hurry! We stayed in hotels, lying about how many cats we had. The hotels would charge per cat, so MBW would walk past the front counter showing the hotel receptionist cute little Moose, and I would sneak the other three through a side or back door, by the last night at a hotel we were professionals at smuggling cats. The drive across the United States was astonishing, farms, miles of green fields, small towns, big cities, crops, American flags flying in every town. Lakes and rivers entrenching our gorgeous country, it was a humbling drive. Thoughts of my past forty years consumed my mind the whole trip.

We made it to New England, twenty two hundred miles, five days, and a lot of gas. Many friends and acquaintances asked us why in the heck would we move out of the beautiful state we lived in, my answer stayed the same; why not? We only have one life to live, I want to see and experience different places in the U.S. and the world. Although our old state is an absolutely amazing state with incredible mountains and outdoor activities it just wasn't for us anymore, it had become over populated and expensive, but a strong growing economy. This is my own opinion! It is a great place to be if you don't mind traffic, and a fast pace life style, it offers a great night life and is good for single young adults looking to have fun.

The part of New England we moved to is slower paced, no traffic, and a better place to raise a family. The only thing I do not like about our fresh start in New England is Tom Brady's face is everywhere, wish he would retire so the Patriots can suck again, oh and sports start late.

Here we are settled in, my house surrounded by thick forest, my son down stairs watching *The Karate Kid*, the four cats perched on window ledges gawking at chipmunks, and my beautiful wife sleeping after a graveyard shift at the animal hospital. This is where I ended up after the first forty. The rest of my story is filled with my life as an American growing up on this earth and the life that has led me to where I am now, I made it; happy, content and ready to begin my next forty.

IDAHO

July 8th, 1976, I was born on an Air Force base in the south. My father was twenty nine at the time and in the Air Force, my mother was eight years younger.

Following our short stay in Biloxi my father was transferred to Clement Falls Oregon. I don't have memories of living in these two states, but what a difference, Mississippi all the way to Oregon. After Oregon he was transferred to Mountain Home Air Force Base Idaho, and here in Idaho is where the memories of my life begin.

We lived in base housing. All the houses looked the same one street to the next; if you were lucky you would have one pine tree in the front yard. It was always dry and windy as far as I can remember. Behind our house there was railroad tracks that ran as far as you can see, the base was in the middle of a desert. Our playground was a F-111 Air Force fighter jet that was on display next to the railroads tracks. My brother and I and several neighborhood kids would play for hours around that jet and throw rocks at each other with no protective gear on. We never had serious injuries, just small bumps and bruises.

Imagine that.

When we weren't playing around the jet, we would play cowboys and Indians. I always played the Indian, I took that game seriously. I felt a spiritual connection when I was an Indian, but for some reason we never won. Thinking back there have always been those kids that you obviously shoot and kill first with your pretend bow and arrow or rifle and they would yell, you missed me, as they ran off down the street. Stunned, I would think to myself, I clearly shot that little bastard first. Honestly, I never was one to cheat at cowboys and Indians, it was never worth the argument. Okay, you killed me, good for you, we have endless lives, it's a game you moron. For hours we would play, and despite the lack of integrity from the cowboys that would never die, it was a blast to maneuver through the neighborhood trying to defeat the enemy.

After everyone died countless times from playing cowboys and Indians we would have a change of pace. Darth Vader, Luke Skywalker, green army men, and many more figurines would be gathered by all the kids and be set to battle in a small dirt depression surrounded by crispy dry grass. There was no good or bad side, we all picked one at a time, you could end up with Darth Vader and Super Man on one side, Luke Skywalker and Jabba the Hut on the other side. There were enough toys to go around. Another kid would take all the green plastic army men and tanks, build a deck or two of bicycle playing cards around them to provide cover and concealment against all of the enemies. What we didn't have yet were cute little Ewoks, Transformers and He-man characters, they didn't join the fight until 1983. All in all, the best part of it all was our imaginations; Darth Vader, Superman and GI Joe would attack Skywalker, Jabba the Hut and Crew. Spiderman, controlled by a kid's hand sailed over Army men shooting webs into the forts of playing cards destroying them at a moment's notice, but not without a rock missile flying out of a tank and amputating both of Spiderman's legs and he would fall helplessly to the feet of Cobra Commander who walked over him as if he were dirt. Lastly, the grand finale, out in a distant gathered behind one of those lonely pine trees in the bare yard gathered three apples high, blue, magic mushroom living Smurfs. Papa Smurf would lead the attack and destroy everyone. There were no rules, we all got along and made up the scenario as the battles and play went on.

In between war of the figurines, we would have classic movies/T.V. shows we could watch time and time again. My first movie I went to was *E.T.*, what an amazing hit. It was released June 11th, 1982, I vividly remember standing in line at the on base movie theatre to get tickets. Back then all you had to choose from was what size soda and popcorn you wanted; no gluten free, low carb, microbrew, calorie counting, fruit appetizer menu. Just a big bucket of buttered and salt drenched popcorn to go along with my large caffeinated Pepsi, yummy. When I saw *E.T.* for the first time I was terrified, he was ugly, but as the movie went on you learned to love him! When he was all gray in color laying by the river looking like a modern-day meth head it was very sad, no one wanted to see him die. The best thing about *E.T.* is, if it's on TV I will watch it, it never gets old. As far as T.V shows I used to love *The A Team*, even with all the explosions no one ever died. Mr. T, Hannibal, Face and Murdock were bad ass dudes, I actually named my first cat Murdock. Another movie I was forced to go to the neighbor's house and watch, was *Children of the Corn*, that movie scared the crap out of me. It was bad enough the movie setting looked somewhat like where we lived. After watching that damn movie I couldn't fall asleep at night, thoughts crowded my mind of crazy children eating corn underneath my bed, and they would wait patiently for me to fall asleep and then sacrifice me. I had this nightmare for years following that movie, I am not sure if it was from watching it or not, but I would dream of three skinny half goblin half teenagers, with long thin hair, teeth like a piano missing keys, they had holey cut off jean shorts that showed areas of their stained tighty whities, bulging blood shot eyes, stripped tube socks covered their wart infested legs to the knee and they wore the original white high-top Nike shoes coated in mud, the shoe laces were half way unlaced. As I stood paralyzed in the kitchen, eyeballing them gnawing on endless corn on the cob, they would periodically turn their awful goblin head, look at me for a split second then return to munching on corn. Needless to say, they were appalling, I used to call them the goblin triplets, I would pray at night that I wouldn't dream of them.

Other movies such as *Star Wars, Indiana Jones, Back to the Future*, and *Airplane*, and so many others from the late seventies and early eighties that will never be forgotten, absolutely great movies. As famous movies were being made along came MTV, and the historical music video *Thriller*. Several mornings before school, the neighbor kids and I would gather together at someone's house and watch *Thriller*, it was as popular as putting a man on the moon in 1969. It was a little scary, but at the same time, rad to watch.

With the release of *Thriller* came the red Michael Jackson jacket, white glove covered in fake bling-bling, and flattened cardboard boxes laid out for moon walking and break-dancing competitions. I swear I was so good at it, my high-top Nike shoes would glide so smooth across the cardboard, as if I were floating on air, my arms and shoulders would wave side to side followed by a tip toe three hundred and sixty degree turn and slight slide to the rear. We all had our distinguished moves, I thought I was 'bad'. What a great past time! Maybe one day MTV will show music videos again, and stop airing nothing but shit reality shows.

Besides playing games, watching movies and T.V shows, I started my sports career as a youth soccer player. Pretty sure all young boy and girls start out with soccer, it seems like the gateway to all sports. Soccer is a lot of running, its tiring at any age, I took the game serious and was very passionate about playing. I remember my first pair of cleats, those cleats made me proud, it felt like I belonged to something, and I loved it. Wish I had pictures, but I am pretty sure I was as cute as a button, I had a pink soccer shirt with nut hugging red shorts all black Nike cleats and bright, blonde hair, I felt important! I only recall one play, but it was the best play. The ball was kicked by one of the opposite team players, and SMACK, it nailed me upside the head. It sent me flying, the crowd sighed in sadness, I quickly gained my senses, got myself to my feet, found the ball, dribbled down the field, shot and scored. It was a play that could have made the ESPN top ten. Unfortunately, that was the only goal my team scored all season.

There I was growing up, an all-American kid, life was great. During those years families seemed to be happy, still to this day I hear how the late seventies and eighties were good times in our country. There was not much to complain about, the media wasn't divided politically as they are today, Ronald Reagan was in office dealing with The Cold War between Russia and U.S. which seemed to have turned out well, we are still here. March 30th, 1981 there was the John Hickey Jr. failed assassination attempt on Reagan.

Two months before that President Reagan in my opinion made one of the most inspirational speeches in history January 20th, 1981,

The Patriotic Speech

If we look to the answer as to why for so many years we achieved so much, prospered as no other people on Earth, it was because here in this land we unleashed the energy and individual genius of man to a greater extent than has ever been done before. Freedom and the dignity of the individual have been more available and assured here than in any other place on Earth. The price for this freedom at times has been high, but we have never been unwilling to pay that price.

It is no coincidence that our present troubles parallel and are proportionate to the intervention and intrusion in our lives that result from unnecessary and excessive growth of government. It is time for us to realize that we're too great a nation to limit ourselves to small dreams. We're not, as some would have us believe, doomed to an inevitable decline. I do not believe in a fate that will fall on us no matter what we do. I do believe in a fate that will fall on us if we do nothing. So, with all the creative energy at our command, let us begin an era of national renewal. Let us renew our determination, our courage, and our strength. And let us renew our faith and our hope.

We have every right to dream heroic dreams. Those who say that we're in a time when there are not heroes, they just don't know where to look. You can see heroes every day going in and out of factory gates. Others, a handful in number, produce enough food to feed all of us and then the world beyond. You meet heroes across a counter, and they're on both sides of that counter. There are entrepreneurs with faith in themselves and faith in an idea who create new jobs, new wealth and opportunity. They're individuals and families whose taxes support the government and whose voluntary gifts support church, charity, culture, art, and education. Their patriotism is quiet, but deep. Their values sustain our national life.

Now, I have used the words "they" and "their" in speaking of these heroes. I could say "you" and "your," because I'm addressing the heroes of whom I speak—you, the citizens of this blessed land. Your dreams, your hopes, your goals are going to be the dreams, the hopes, and the goals of this administration, so help me God.

We shall reflect the compassion that is so much a part of your makeup. How can we love our country and not love our countrymen; and loving them, reach out a hand when they fall, heal them when they're sick, and provide opportunity to make them self-sufficient so they will be equal in fact and not just in theory?

Can we solve the problems confronting us? Well, the answer is an unequivocal and emphatic "yes." To paraphrase Winston Churchill, I did not take the oath I've just taken with the intention of presiding over the dissolution of the world's strongest economy.

In the days ahead I will propose removing the roadblocks that have slowed our economy and reduced productivity. Steps will be taken aimed at restoring the balance between the various levels of government. Progress may be slow, measured in inches and feet, not miles, but we will progress. It is time to reawaken this industrial giant, to get government back within its means, and to lighten our punitive tax burden. And these will be our first priorities, and on these principles there will be no compromise.

On the eve of our struggle for independence a man who might have been one of the greatest among the Founding Fathers, Dr. Joseph Warren, president of the Massachusetts Congress, said to his fellow Americans, "Our country is in danger, but not to be despaired of . . . . On you depend the fortunes of America. You are to decide the important questions upon which rests the happiness and the liberty of millions yet unborn. Act worthy of yourselves."

Well, I believe we, the Americans of today, are ready to act worthy of ourselves, ready to do what must be done to ensure happiness and liberty for ourselves, our children, and our children's children. And as we renew ourselves here in our own land, we will be seen as having greater strength throughout the world. We will again be the exemplar of freedom and a beacon of hope for those who do not now have freedom.

To those neighbors and allies who share our freedom, we will strengthen our historic ties and assure them of our support and firm commitment. We will match loyalty with loyalty. We will strive for mutually beneficial relations. We will not use our friendship to impose on their sovereignty, for our own sovereignty is not for sale.

As for the enemies of freedom, those who are potential adversaries, they will be reminded that peace is the highest aspiration of the American people. We will negotiate for it, sacrifice for it; we will not surrender for it, now or ever.

Our forbearance should never be misunderstood. Our reluctance for conflict should not be misjudged as a failure of will. When action is required to preserve our national security, we will act. We will maintain sufficient strength to prevail if need be, knowing that if we do so we have the best chance of never having to use that strength.

Above all, we must realize that no arsenal or no weapon in the arsenals of the world is so formidable as the will and moral courage of free men and women. It is a weapon our adversaries in today's world do not have. It is a weapon that we as Americans do have. Let that be understood by those who practice terrorism and prey upon their neighbors.

I'm told that tens of thousands of prayer meetings are being held on this day, and for that I'm deeply grateful. We are a nation under God, and I believe God intended for us to be free. It would be fitting and good, I think, if on each Inaugural Day in future years it should be declared a day of prayer.

This is the first time in our history that this ceremony has been held, as you've been told, on this West Front of the Capitol. Standing here, one faces a magnificent vista, opening up on this city's special beauty and history. At the end of this open mall are those shrines to the giants on whose shoulders we stand.

Directly in front of me, the monument to a monumental man, George Washington, father of our country. A man of humility who came to greatness reluctantly. He led America out of revolutionary victory into infant nationhood. Off to one side, the stately memorial to Thomas Braxerson. The Declaration of Independence flames with his eloquence. And then, beyond the Reflecting Pool, the dignified columns of the Lincoln Memorial. Whoever would understand in his heart the meaning of America will find it in the life of Abraham Lincoln.

Beyond those monuments to heroism is the Potomac River, and on the far shore the sloping hills of Arlington National Cemetery, with its row upon row of simple white markers bearing crosses or Stars of David. They add up to only a tiny fraction of the price that has been paid for our freedom.

Each one of those markers is a monument to the kind of hero I spoke of earlier. Their lives ended in places called Belleau Wood, The Argonne, Omaha Beach, Salerno, and halfway around the world on Guadalcanal, Tarawa, Pork Chop Hill, the Chosin Reservoir, and in a hundred rice paddies and jungles of a place called Vietnam.

Under one such marker lies a young man, Martin Treptow, who left his job in a small town barbershop in 1917 to go to France with the famed Rainbow Division. There, on the western front, he was killed trying to carry a message between battalions under heavy artillery fire.

We're told that on his body was found a diary. On the flyleaf under the heading, "My Pledge," he had written these words:

"America must win this war. Therefore I will work, I will save, I will sacrifice, I will endure, I will fight cheerfully and do my utmost, as if the issue of the whole struggle depended on me alone."

The crisis we are facing today does not require of us the kind of sacrifice that Martin Treptow and so many thousands of others were called upon to make. It does require, however, our best effort and our willingness to believe in ourselves and to believe in our capacity to perform great deeds, to believe that together with God's help we can and will resolve the problems which now confront us.

And after all, why shouldn't we believe that? We are Americans.

God bless you, and thank you.

I love that speech, it makes me love our great country more and more every time I hear or read it.

Other events that happened during this time was the May 18th, 1980 Mount St. Helen eruption in Skamania County, Washington. Our vehicles, yards, and houses were blanketed by ash all the way in Idaho, it was as if it snowed. The volcanic eruption destroyed two hundred and thirty square miles of forest, claimed fifty seven lives. December 8th 1980, the great Beatle, John Lennon, was murdered outside his apartment by Mark David Chapman.

Those were the times I remember in Idaho. In the next few years my dad had been transferred to Lowry Air Force Base Colorado, just on the border of Denver. My parents had bought a house out in the economy, we were no longer in base housing, I was excited, it was freedom to live off of a military base. We were finally in the real world, and so the first forty continues in Aurora, Colorado.

EAGLE

As I began to write my rough draft about the eighties, I found a great place to write. My wife traveled to Orlando for a veterinarian conference and I tagged along. It was winter in most states, but sunny Orlando was a perfect seventy five degrees. We were able to watch the Eagles beat the Patriots in Super Bowl LII. First time as far as I can remember watching a Super Bowl sober, and remarkably it was damn good entertainment. Justin Timberlake had an outstanding performance, no kneeling during the National Anthem, and the Patriots didn't cheat, or did they? Noone cared because they lost.

The following morning, Monday, February 5th, 2018, well rested, feeling great, I went on a jog, which was so much easier at sea level than running at a mile high in Denver where there is no oxygen. I had a delicious breakfast from Denny's, my wife was at her conference, I relaxed all day, listened to Pandora and wrote more of the first forty.

Transitioning from an Air force base to living out on the economy in civilian life was not so bad. As kids we always worry about meeting new friends, going to a new school, and hoping we fit in, but it's not always as bad as we think.

The house my parents purchased was walking distance to all the schools, elementary through high school, and we lived off of a big park, it was a very convenient location. The house was small but just right for the four of us. My dad had cousins that lived nearby, we would spend some weekends at their place riding dirt bikes. Our neighbors had three boys that were mine and my brothers age, that was a huge plus, we quickly made friends, and everyone knew who the new kids on the block were, figuratively speaking.

Everything was changing so fast, we moved, I started elementary school, started playing basketball in a youth league. Go Spartans! I was living a typical American lifestyle, at least I thought I was. I was a kid, naïve to the world, I just wanted to play sports, eat pizza, go to school, watch real eighties cartoons on Saturday mornings, play Nintendo and hang out with friends. We would have pick up football games at the park. It took one kid to call a friend on the land line or actually walk to a kid's house to get them to come out and play a game of football. We would play for hours without pads, no flags, no touch football, just hard core tackling, and everyone walked home with minor bruises, sprained joints and an occasional black eye, but no major injuries. If we weren't playing football we were playing basketball on those gravel covered elementary school courts that had those annoying metal nets, but we managed and had good games. We would play until the street lights came on. Along with playing sports, I enjoyed riding my Target huffy bike over to friend's house to play the new Nintendo. That gray box was awesome, we had an Atari 2600, but the Nintendo, holy shit, what a break through! Neighborhood gamers figured out how to get endless lives playing *Super Mario Brothers*. I just googled how you can get extra lives and it your ass is old, hahaha! There were also games such as *Legend of Zelda*, which was too much thinking. So I stuck with *Contra, Duck Hunt* and games like *Mike Tysons Punch Out*, it took me about six months, but I beat Mikes ass. I went through Little Mac all the way to Macho Man to fight 'Mighty' Mike Tyson.

As far as professional sports, everyone in my new home town were of course Bronco fans, Elway had just joined the league, but so did Dan Marino. While everyone was praising the Broncos, I had become a die-hard Dolphins fan. Why Miami you might ask? My dream was to be a Marine Biologist, therefore I loved dolphins. I had dolphin sweats, bed sheets, dolphin stuffed animals, I had everything dolphins.

I had good friend who supported the Chicago Bears, I spent a lot of time at his house. We would watch football and order Dominos Pizza. Dominos tasted different back then for some reason, it was better tasting than present day pizza, not sure why! Anyways, the Miami Dolphins and the Bears played one of the best Monday Night Football games in history. December 2nd, 1985 the Dolphins beat the Bears thirty eight to twenty four to end the Bears perfect season. Although the Bears had their first and only loss of the season they went to win the Super Bowl, and the Super Bowl Shuffle was created.

Life wasn't just about sports and Nintendo, I was in the fifth grade when tragedy struck our space program. I remember sitting in my classroom, the teacher and all my classmates were watching the NASA shuttle orbiter mission STS-51-L. The tenth mission for the Space Shuttle Challenger. Seventy three seconds into its flight it broke apart, killing five astronauts and two payload specialists. The explosion happened over Cape Canaveral Florida on January 28th, 1986. The country was stunned, many schools, if not all throughout the country, were tuned into that shuttle launch, and knowing there was a school teacher on that flight, made it more disturbing.

We were huddled in a horseshoe around the tube T.V when our teacher turned the dial to off. Kids slowly and silently made their way to their seats. The rest of the day was sad.

Being in elementary school I think it added higher emotions, we still loved space/stars, airplanes, the world, we were humble children. As humans, if you are not directly affected by tragedy we are programmed to forget as time goes on. I haven't forgot them!

They were heroes to me; risking their lives to bring education to the human race, wearing the American Flag proudly as they boarded the shuttle, and most of all leaving their families knowing there was a high risk of what they were about to encounter, but unselfishly doing their mission for us to learn more about space and Haley's Comet. The United States of America always comes together and always will when tragedy happens. Yes! The Challenger was a tragic event, we should always keep those great Americans in our heart and in our schools.

Shit! What's next? I am looking for a transition word into my next paragraph. I found it!

Shit. So there I was, about to graduate sixth grade, but before I start continuing my story, I have to tell about my first crush.

I will call my first crush dimples. This was the first time I had that 'feeling' about a girl, all you boys know what I am talking about! She was so cute on the swing, strawberry blonde hair, dimples the size of a pimples when she smiled, ahh I was in love. So, with that being said, I had one of my friends go ask her to be my girlfriend, and that boomerang came back to me in seconds.

"No," she said. I was hurt and embarrassed, that was the first time I was rejected by a girl, but I needed to move on, I took it like a man.

Although the whole dating scene wasn't working in my favor, elementary school was still fun. During recess and lunch most kids would play football, basketball, or we would gather around one of the popular kids and he would tell us the new dirty word he heard from his parents or the older kids. Yes parents; your kids do repeat what you say and mirror how you act. I don't want to share some of the nasty words I learned at that age, but I am sure everyone has a good idea. At the elementary school, my brother and I met some good people that I still stay in touch with to this day. We grew up with a family that had three kids. Their oldest boy and my brother were three years older than me. Their daughter was my age and the other son was three years younger than me. Our parents would hang out from time to time and watch football, my brother became really close to the older brother and they remained good friends throughout high school. The daughter and I knew each other, but we really never hung out, Dimples was her best friend so I wasn't popular with them. However her and I have had small talk throughout the years thanks to Myspace and Facebook. The two brothers, even though there was a five or six year gap between the two, were very close, and popular, I looked up to them, they were good looking boys. The oldest, Hawk, was in sixth grade I was in fourth and the youngest brother, Eagle, was in first. I remember when Eagle first came to the school, Hawk was proud of him, they dressed alike wearing bright, Bermuda shorts, colorful short sleeve button up shirts, not one hundred percent sure what shoes they wore, but if I were a betting man I would say Vans. Nonetheless, they were pretty rad, and I am glad I got to know them.

The reason I write about this all-American family is because of the youngest brother, Eagle. Jumping ahead to when I was a Senior, Hawk, told me to watch over Eagle when he came into high school as a freshman. I took his request seriously, I wouldn't let anyone harm him at all, but it wasn't that difficult of a task, Eagle was a great kid, very kind, shy, and athletic.

Again, jumping ahead; thirteen years after my graduation from high school it was May 2007. Routine night in Iraq, I was working a night shift inside a medevac compound, my job was to fuel medevac Blackhawk helicopters as they returned from extracting injured or Killed in Action Soldier throughout Iraq. That night a radio call came across the net for a downed medic attached to a Ranger Battalion. The Blackhawk completed the mission and landed back at the medevac compound. Another Soldier and I drove the fuel truck over to the Blackhawk to refuel it, as we stood by waiting for the fuel to stop, I glanced inside the Blackhawk, there were dark wet spots scattered throughout the floor of the Blackhawk, medical bandages were stained with blood, this wasn't training anymore, this was real life war.

We finished the refuel process and headed back to our staging area, our shift was finished it was early morning I had been up all night, I ate breakfast and fell fast asleep. Hours later I woke up and walked over to the internet cafe to check my email and messages. I had a message from back home in Colorado, a good friend who sadly told me about the death of Eagle in Iraq, I put two and two together and realized that haunting scene from the Blackhawk last night was that of Eagles. Shocked, I later confirmed the Soldier name and it was Eagle on that Blackhawk. I felt instantly helpless, there was nothing I could do! Childhood memories of him flooded my mind, I asked God and myself, why do bad things happen to great people? I kept it to myself, I had Soldier under me that I didn't want to be emotional in front of, I mourned alone. I cried silently in my bunk for Eagle and his family, I prayed for them, and prayed for the rest of us to get home safely. He was supposed to go home in a few weeks to see the birth of his baby, but he never made it. He made the ultimate sacrifice for his family and our beloved country. You and your family will forever be in my heart. I am sure he is watching over his family and all of his brotherhood from Heaven above. I wanted to tell Eagles story early on in my book, he deserves the utmost respect. Love you guys!

Leaping back to the late eighties, I left my career as a soccer player and fell in love with basketball. I played for a youth league called Spartans, and being the new kid to the neighborhood I was put on a team that has never played together, and we didn't know each other.

Most teams had been playing together for a few years, but as far as our team that was not the situation. All in all, I loved it, once again I was on a team, just like my soccer team, my basketball team sucked as well, we lost every game, every season, but no matter what I would never leave my teammates. Although we lost a lot, I had a great coach I will never forget. He worked at the local supermarket in the meat department. One night at practice, he pulled me aside, kneeled down, and told me to relax!

"You are a leader and you will go far in life," he said. I still remember him speaking those words to me to this day. Coaches, teachers, and any other profession that inspire and influence our children in a positive manner are incredible, and highly patient individuals. I will always support them, unless they are crazy as hell of course.

Here I go again trying to find a way to transition into another paragraph to end chapter three, but screw it, I like this way of transitioning better, not sure if its correct or not. Anyways, I graduated from sixth grade, I was moving on, growing up fast, but I was ready for seventh grade, and as I keep writing I get more and more excited, I love this!

I have to add something to my book; It's September 10th, 2018, my wife and I are watching Monday Night Football, she is pregnant, and I am happy as all can be about our new addition, she keeps tooting while at the same time looking at me laughing.

She says in her cute voice, "I can't help it, it's baby moose farting." We don't know the sex of the baby yet, but she loves moose, we have a cat named moose, so it's baby moose until we know.

Enough of present time, and back to the seventh grade. I have no complaints up to now.

As I grow and mature, life is about to get a little off track, but as humans don't we sometimes fall off track? It's how we get back on track that matters.

SMOKING AND DRINKING

Seventh grade was an innocent year for me, I did my homework, made good grades, met a lot of other kids from different schools and was still fitting in just fine. However, a couple of friends and I from my elementary school got suspended toward the end of seventh grade for throwing those stink bombs you get from Spencer's gift shop down hallways and specifically into the music teachers' classroom, the whole school smelled like rotten eggs, other than that I sailed right along to the summer between seventh and eighth grade.

Summer days consisted of watching The Price is Right, some re-runs of *Leave It To Beaver* on channel two, and waiting on a friend to call me on my landline to go to the public pool for only one dollar, play basketball or just hang out and play Nintendo, I now actually call it No-friendo.

Summer evenings were fun as well. Several friends, both boys and girls would meet at one of our houses and one of the parents would drive us to the movie theatre or bowling alley. I regret it now, but I was embarrassed if my parents drove us because we had a rusted out 1977 Nova. I wish I didn't care about my image so much as a teenager, it really doesn't get you anywhere.

What sucked the most, is when we would go out nearly all my friends had girlfriends, I always felt like the odd man out. I had greasy hair, shoulders that looked like it snowed on them from the dandruff that fell out of my hair, zits covered my chin, back and chest and to top it all off I was a little chubby, I had little if any self-confidence and very low self-esteem as well. Basically, I felt like I was following my friends around trying to fit in, I wasn't a very happy kid around this time in my life. To add to my unhappiness, I would go home and my parents were constantly fighting, I would hide under the covers and pray that they would stop because the arguments got so loud, I usually ended up asking to stay at a friends house. (Please parents don't fight like this in front of your kids, they are scared and love you both unconditionally)

Before I continue I just have to say I hold nothing against my parents, they were separated and divorced when I was fifteen, but they had to do what was best for them, and they are both very happy.

Continuing on, and not so innocent anymore, some kids and I were walking down the street, it was a weekday, so obviously all of the adults were at work, or they should've been, so we were not worried about being seen. Anyways, one of the kids broke out a pack of cigarettes, and of course asked if anyone wanted to try one, and without hesitation I said hell yeah. I lit it, but like Bill Clinton I didn't inhale (and yes I know he said that about weed, but just keep reading), it wasn't until the fourth or fifth cigarette that I did inhale, and damn, did I cough. Despite the cough and choking on smoke I loved the high or buzz from the nicotine coursing through my veins, it was something I never felt before. I was uneducated, and naïve about smoking, and really didn't care at that age, but looking back I wish I would have never done it. The important thing is that I am nicotine free now, and I will always be open about it towards my kids to show them the dangers of it and hope they make the right decisions.

Here I was, a young addict, greasy head, pizza face, but I was starting to feel happy, my self-confidence was building. I became a regular smoker and kids called me the Marlboro man, uggghhhh like I said, WHAT THE HELL WAS I THINKING? My dad would come home and I would be smoking out the window in my bedroom, thinking I could cover the smell with matches, again, WHAT THE HELL WAS I THINKING? You can smell cigarette smoke a mile away. Back then it was easy to get addicted to nicotine, no one carded. I would walk to 7-11 and get a slurpee, a pack of Marlboro Reds, and a free pack of matches for a total of two dollars and nineteen cents. To add to the convenience of smoking, there was a deli owned by a gentleman and his family from Europe or the Middle East, back then I didn't know the difference, he would sell me those little cancer sticks as well. I would tell my parents I was going to a friend's house on Saturday mornings but really would go to their deli to get smokes. So, it started, I was thirteen, I had become a smoker, and I convinced myself, if I smoke I might as well drink.

Drinking was easy as well. My dad being in the Air Force would have get-togethers with his fellow Airmen, and a keg of beer was always present. Being the intelligent teens we thought we were, my best friend and I, would patiently wait for an hour or so, and then it was like ants stealing sugar at a picnic. When the coast was clear we would rush out to the garage where the keg was, fill up our solo cups and stash them behind Quaker state oil bottles on a bench. We would stroll back inside and show our presence, saying hi to all the adults, who were clueless about what our mission was, but we didn't know that. Basically, everyone was naïve. This was a three-part mission; one, poor the beer and stash it; two, show our face and act like we gave a shit about talking to my dads' friends; three, when the garage was clear, we would go out grab the solo cups full of our stashed beer, scramble out the back door of the garage, into a dark corner of the backyard and drink, giggle and high five each other like we just out smarted all the stupid grown-ups.

After the party died down and people left to go home; obviously no Lyft, Uber, probably no seatbelts either, our buzz would slowly wear off, but that was okay because we had *The Simpsons* to watch or *Mike Tysons Punch Out* to conquer.

That week, remnants of stale keg beer, and vodka hung around, so of course I had to be the popular one in the neighborhood and invite kids over to finish the leftovers, nothing like drinking hot keg beer on a July summer day. It wasn't about the taste, it was about that numb feeling, the uncontrollable laughter, and I am not going to lie, it was fun at the time. We would hang out on my back deck drinking beer, smoking Marlboro's and forcing down shots of straight vodka. I felt like a grown up, I even learned how to BBQ at this time. A smoke, a drink, and a spatula in hand, what else could a kid want? Yes, we were wrong as hell for doing the things we did at that age, and in no means am I promoting this kind of behavior for any kid, but damn it was fun at that time. It was not worth it in the long run, and again I am honest with my son about my past behavior, only to educate him on what not to do.

I was never worried if my dad noticed the keg beer slowly getting drained, not sure that he even paid attention to it, but the vodka, that was obvious something was different about it. Being the intelligent kid, I was, after taking shots I would replace it with water. Eventually it wasn't vodka anymore it was a bottle of water, fortunately nothing was ever said, maybe my parents didn't drink vodka. That was the extent of the summer between my seventh and eighth grade year, I was rapidly building a reputation.

As I move on into my eighth grade year, I mentioned earlier about writing on vacations, or weekend getaways, but this time I continued my book from home, and as I wrote, I watched the 2018 winter Olympics in Korea, and the U.S Women's Hockey Team beat Canada for the Gold, great job ladies! Moving on in life, eighth grade was about to start, I was young, dumb, and cocky, but I knew no better.

ICEMAN

Eighth grade started, we were still doing movie nights on weekends, and one of those nights was a night to remember. It was my first kiss ever, but the way it happened wasn't the most dignified time in my life.

I began the night dating a girl, who I will call K1, we walked into the movie theatre hand in hand, I liked K1 a lot. That same day at school during math class, I had a girl that I will call K2, she sent me a note that passed five or six different hands to get back to me in the back of the class; not a text! It was notebook paper folded up in a small square with a heart on the outside, and I was more excited to open that note than any text I have ever had on a cell phone. I can't honestly remember exactly what the note said, but it basically said she thought I was cute, which was huge for me, I needed that from a cute girl.

Back to that night, I was with K1, when K2 showed up with friends, and all I can remember was sitting against the wall inside the movie theatre holding hands and kissing K2, I don't even remember the movie we were watching, it might have been *Honey I Shrunk The Kids*. K1 was mad as hell, and I felt like a total jerk, but I didn't know how to act at that age, I was young and not thinking, this was all new to me.

The night ended with K1 being pissed and K2 was my girlfriend. Come Monday at school it was awkward, K2 and I walked around the hallways of the school holding hands during lunch, occasionally passing K1, that is what kids did that were dating back then, no phones, or internet, just personal time talking with each other.

Throughout the year nothing changed, I quickly left K2 for AM, then cheated on AM with MM, and had a one-night kissing session with TA, but stayed with MM, and finally ended with SS, which didn't last long at all. Yeah, it's nothing to brag about, I think back and realize what a little punk I was, and wish I would have stayed with K1. All this dating was innocent, strictly holding hands and kissing, nothing more, but present day if I were a politician, actor or president I would be up shit creek, I would have the media on me like flies on shit for having innocent childhood relationships, the FBI would probably find love notes with hearts that were sent back and forth between me and girlfriends and I would have to testify for being a fourteen-year-old boy who liked girls.

Anyway, I met up with K1 twenty seven years later at a local bar, and she told me that night pissed her off. Of course, she was right, I was a dick. The ironic thing about that whole night is that the movie theatre we were at is now a church, how symbolic of my life. She also reminded me of how I dressed, and acted in eighth grade; jeans or bugle boy pants slightly lowered so you can see my boxers hanging out. The bottom of my jeans were folded over and rolled, my shoes were either vans or basketball shoes, a buttoned up shirt with the long sleeves rolled to mid forearm, and a white Miami Hurricanes hat that on the side I had wrote Iceman. Sure, the hat was stupid, but that is what my friends and I did. I cannot remember what their nicknames were on their hat, but it was probably like Maverick, and G-Man, or something close in nature.

Now that my popularity with the girls and fellow eighth graders was growing, I was on a roll. Always had a girlfriend, I could get alcohol and cigarettes, kids liked me for all the wrong reasons, but I didn't care. I was invited to classmates houses when their parents were out of town, I brought beer, a bottle of vodka and cigarettes. One of those invites was at a kid's house who was a news anchor for Fox. To make a long story short, we partied at his house, I kissed TA for hours, who was dating a muscled, long-haired scary popular guy, but I wasn't skeeered! Kids puked under the pool table, the house was trashed, and damnit, he ratted us out. His mom called my parents, she must have used the white pages to get our number, and my mom was pissed at me, but it didn't last long.

Every time I see him on TV, I think back to that day and get a little irritated, asking myself how are you going to blame everyone else for your stupid decisions? I was just invited to have fun, and now I am the guilty one because he wouldn't take responsibility for his actions; but who am I to judge? I probably would have ratted kids out as well. Oh well, I am over it.

Along with being a smoking, beer drinking, zit faced punk, who for some reason had a lot of girlfriends, I still managed to play basketball. Basketball was a release for me. Being one of the better players in eighth grade I was picked to play on the teachers versus students game. TA was in the audience, and at a one point I heard her yell, nice legs Brodee, hearing her say that sent my ego sky high, so high that I started mouthing off to teachers and got thrown out. Who gets thrown out of a teacher versus student game? Apparently, I do! Life was still good, I closed out eighth grade and the beginning of summer with parties, girls, beer, smokes, and to add to the excitement, we were blessed with music that is still around to this day; Motley Crew, Run DMC, Aerosmith, Poison, NWA, and Alabama, just to name a few. I could keep going for days.

Proceeding my glorious eighth grade year, a lot of my friends were split into two high schools. Another school had opened that year which gave students and parents a choice on which school to join. Unfortunately, that resulted in losing friends. Regardless, I quickly jumped into two-a-day practices preparing for freshman year football, and being the first time I have ever played organized football, it was very strenuous. Not to mention, the Taco Bell diet, hot and dry summer days probably didn't assist in my ass beating practice every day, but I loved every moment of it.

Along with moving on in life, our world was changing as well. That summer of 1990 the Berlin wall was totally demolished, there are many questions who was responsible for the actual destruction. On June 12th, 1987 President Reagan spoke the famous words "Tear down this wall", referring to the leader of the Soviet Union Mikhail Gorbachev, the wall had divided East and West Berlin since 1961. Finally, after twenty nine years of families being apart, Germany was united as one. At that time in 1990 I never thought that I would be in Germany five years later.

LUCY IN THE SKY WITH DIAMONDS

Freshman year began. I was dating JC, we actually lasted a few months, I was getting better at the whole dating scene, but JC was the last girlfriend for the remainder of my high school years. I also maintained a GPA of 3.667, played on the freshman basketball, and football team, loved homecoming, pride week and pep-rallies. All that pride I had only lasted about half a semester. Not sure when all hell broke loose, but for the next two years it was a wild ride.

Pretty sure my wildness started when sports ended for me during winter time. I smoked more cigarettes, drank more liquor and beer, and was attending any and every party possible.

Although I regret these two years of my life, I can't turn back time, so I accept the dumb shit I did and I moved on. The dumb shit I did for those two years were not the smartest decisions, but no one is perfect.

Every Friday night, high school kids would meet at a local fast food place parking lot. We would find out which brave ass kid wanted to have a party at their house while their parents were gone for the weekend. If we couldn't find a house to party at, then we would party train out East. (Party train definition: Many under age high school students driving in a long convoy with parent bought vehicles out to a secluded location to drink keg beer, do hippie drugs and have a bonfire.)

One of those keg parties out in the boonies turned into a bloody mess for me. Everyone was partying having fun, dancing, listening to loud music that echoed from some rich kids fifteen inch sub woofers. While all this fun was going on, cops were slowly moving in, and just like that our party area lit up like a lightning strike in a cave. Helicopters were shining spot lights downs, red and blue sirens were closing in fast, and my heartbeat was in unison with my mind. I quickly found my best friend, we both agreed to flee on foot. It was pitch black. We focused on street lights that seemed miles away, I could hear cattle but could not see them, and as fast as I was running is as fast that I came to a dead stop. I managed to run full speed into a barb wire fence. As I hit the wire, all four of my limbs were punctured with multiple spikes. My abdomen and chest were lacerated sideways somehow, it looked and felt like Freddy Krueger took a slice at me. I laid motionless swaying back and forth on the wire, the spikes digging deeper. I was in shock. I couldn't even find it in me to yell curse words, and I must have been faster than my friend because he didn't run into anything, sometimes it pays to be the turtle! This was the first time in my life I actually was scared of death, but I wasn't ready for death, and I wasn't ready to get arrested at the age of fourteen.

So here I go; slowly I started to do a modified push-up, pushing myself away from the wire I could feel each spike individually being removed from my skin. The last part was my hands, I pulled my hands back and the wire followed until finally the barbs popped out of my palms, blood began to leak out of each puncture of my body, my chest and stomach were covered in red, but we had to keep moving. I removed my shirt, used it as cushion to straddle the wire to get over it and rapidly walked toward the street lights swinging my bloody shirt in front of us to avoid another fence. We made it to the road, and miraculously a sweet girl from the party who was by herself picked us up. I didn't know her, but knew of her, she didn't ask us any questions, she just said get in, I will take you guys home. The ride home was about ten minutes, not much was said, she dropped us off at my house, we quietly let ourselves in, I took my clothes off and hid them until I could trash them later. It was hard to hide the wounds for weeks, and my stomach wounds were there for years, until I started to develop a beer belly, and they slowly stretched out, but they are still there to today.

Moving on to the second half of freshman year, my grades were slipping, I was goofing off in class, ditching class and took a path toward destruction.

Remember a few pages back when I mentioned Bill Clinton about not inhaling? In his defense I didn't inhale weed the first time I smoked either. It was harsh as heck, but come on Bill, the next time, and the time after, and so on I inhaled like crazy, just be honest, hahaha. Also, who would have thought after all these years it would be legal in most states and Canada ehh.

Now that I was a regular pot smoker, every morning on the way to school I would walk to my best friend's house, we would smoke a joint and then walk a couple blocks to the school. My first period was pre-algebra, no I wasn't good at math, and of course I had to sit in the back of the class. One of those high mornings in class there was a black kid named Marion who sat next to me in class.

He whispered over to me, "Brodee watch this shit". He would put a handful of skittles in his mouth, chew them up really good, but not swallow, there would be a piece of paper on his desk, and he would slowly let the rainbow-colored spit bungee down to the paper, the skittle spit would stick to the paper and he would suck it up to his face. I freaking lost it that morning with uncontrollable laughter and had to leave class. We were immature, but it was damn hilarious at the time. Boys will be boys. I guess if you are going to be a screw up, might as well have fun doing it. I finished freshman year and was slowly spiraling downhill, and then I tried LSD. That sped up my downhill spiral, I was falling fast with no brakes. For the first time in my life I found myself praying to God, not for forgiveness, but for the strength to get through the next twelve hours after taking LSD. Yes, not even fifteen years old yet, and I was trying big time drugs.

Those twelve hours began when I was hanging out with the neighbor boys in our back yard. Street lights had come on, it was a beautiful, warm summer night. All of us guys were high from smoking weed. Then came the LSD, they were small squares of paper with little pink elephants stamped on them. As I stood there and briefly stared at it the tiny square, I asked myself, how much damage could a little piece of paper do to me? Of course, without hesitation I stuck it on my tongue and let it dissolve, it had a distinct taste. I can't think of anything in the world that I could compare the taste with.

Two hours passed, and nothing had happened, I decided to go inside and go to bed.

BAM! As soon as I walked through my front door it hit me, I was officially trippin'. My cat met me at the door, he meowed in waves, the white walls rolled like the ocean. I quickly headed to the basement that was dark and creepy, it reminded me of a medieval dungeon. It was hard to believe all of this hallucination was from that damn pink elephant, I was rocked.

My brother was never home and his room was in the downstairs away from my parents, so that's where I decided to hang out until the high wore off. My brother chewed tobacco, and would spit it on the floor, the carpet was a dark brown so one could not see the stains, but damn it smelt like shit. We both had waterbeds, those were popular in the eighties, not sure why they slowly went away.

Next to the water bed was a grey Sony stereo system, with three-foot-tall speakers, double cassette tape, equalizer, and a turntable for records. It would shake the house. I put "The Wall" by Pink Floyd on the record player and sat down in a worn-out red love seat. It was so worn it formed to your body as you sat in it. On the wall was a poster of Samantha Fox (super model from the eighties), she was in a bathing suit. I looked at the poster and she began to come to life and talk to me. It was magical for a fourteen-year-old boy who's hormones were raging, but that was the extent of that. She was beautiful and every boy's heartthrob, I am sure teenaged girls loved Johnny Depp, Cory Heart and Tom Cruise back then. Back then it was innocent, today it's a sin. After my short date with Samantha Fox, my LSD took me to a concert, Iron Maiden and AC/DC were on posters as well. They came to life and started singing Pink Floyd. They were flinging their eighties hair, they played their instruments and it sounded as though they were actually playing Floyd. I guess that is why they call LSD trippin'. All while this was going on my cat just sat there and stared at me with faint meows like he knew what was going on, I believe animals can sense our feelings and inner thoughts.

The next event of the night was becoming brave enough to go to the kitchen and heat up some left-over pizza in the microwave. So, I began my adventure, I quietly, (or what I thought was quiet), creeped up the stairs to the kitchen, grabbed a few slices and placed them in the microwave, and holy crap, I never seen a machine that was so difficult. For the life of me I couldn't figure out how to work the damn thing, and it was as simple as turning a dial for time and pushing a big black button that said START. Still struggling, my mom came downstairs, and my heart raced, reaching speeds of a rabbit which is about three hundred beats per minute.

"Everything okay?" she calmly asked.

I answered with a scratchy voice. "Yep, just wondering why the microwave won't work".

Without any other words spoke, she walks overs and simply turned it on, then turned around and walked back upstairs. My heart beat went back to normal and I strutted downstairs with my pizza acting like I was smooth as ice, all the time thinking my parents don't know shit.

Back to the chew infested dungeon, I sat down and ate my pizza. I bit in to the deliciousness of left-over Domino's, and unfortunately as I chewed the pizza the LSD told my brain my teeth were falling out. I couldn't tell the difference between pizza crust and my teeth. To calm my mind of the situation, I went and studied my teeth in the mirror, I must have looked them up, down, side to side for over an hour it seemed, but in reality, it was probably like thirty seconds. Luckily, my teeth were still intact, and pretty sure that is the one and only time I threw away pizza in my life.

Apparently this high was not going away, I was still comfortably numb. I decided to head to my own room where I could lay in my waterbed and sleep this drug away. My room was right next to my parents, so I silently burrowed myself into bed and lied there for hours. Scared, and praying that the LSD would wear off soon, I managed to fall asleep, and I woke up to sobriety and the sun shining on my face. I thanked God that morning, and asked him for his forgiveness for being a fool. One would think after an experience like that, it would be the last time, but it wasn't.

The following weekend I stayed at a good friend's house and we ate LSD again. This would be the second time I tried LSD, but this time I was prepared and educated on what was to come.

Waiting on the effects of the LSD to kick in, we lounged in my buddy's room passing joints and smoking cigarettes. We had Alabama playing on the stereo. I asked one of our friends for a lighter, and without reaction, a silver zippo lighter came flying toward my face. At that moment I knew the LSD had kicked in. The lighter came at me in slow motion, but in reality, it was moving so fast it parted the smoked filled room. I watched it all the way to my hand trying to grab it but missed terribly, and wham, that zippo lighter hit me right in the front tooth. Twenty nine years later I still have that chip in my tooth. The Alabama country music, me missing part of my tooth, made us feel like we were all truck drivers, that was the theme that night for the long LSD trip.

I took LSD time and time again, not realizing what it was doing to me. I didn't know who I was. One day I wanted to wear cowboy boots, the next day I wanted to wear leather and be a stoner, and in between all that I wanted to be a jock and play sports.

Thankfully, but scary, my time had come to stop, I believe it was God telling me to stop or you are going to die.

Every time I hear "This is the End" by Jim Morrison and The Doors, I reflect back to the last night I ever did LSD. We were over at a friend's house, I had eaten a tab of LSD, and was smoking bong hits of weed. Within minutes I began to freak out. I had to leave the house in a hurry. I felt so dehydrated from fifteen kids filling the room with weed and cigarette smoke. When I made it outside, I scrambled all over the yard in panic looking for a water hose, I finally found a hose and began to chug water. I was so bloated but I just kept drinking and drinking not knowing that a person can actually drown themselves from drinking water like that, but I was so high I didn't know what I was doing. Then all the sudden something switched in my brain and I had thoughts and feelings of swallowing my tongue. It was the worst feeling I have ever dealt with up to this time in my life. All my friends were so high they thought I was just having a bad trip, well duh, I was having a horrible trip. The rest of the night I held my tongue with my hand. I didn't let go. I could still feel trails of my tongue going back into my throat, so I needed my hand on my tongue to physically know that it wasn't actually happening.

A few buddies and I made it to one of their houses, they went to sleep, I sat motionless on the couch holding my tongue, praying once again to God that I will never do drugs again if you get me through this night. Everywhere I looked in my buddy's house that night I saw images of the devil, snakes, horns, blood and skeletons. I told myself Brodee Reed, this is the last fucking time, I was pissed at myself, I hated who I was.

Morning came, the sun was out once again, I survived. I left my friend's house and began my long walk home, stopping by the gas station to grab a Coke and a pack of Marlboro's. On the way home, I felt like a loser, it was a very low point in my young life, but I was determined, and I never took another piece of the devil's paper (LSD) again.

Although my trippin' days were over, I still drank, and smoked both weed and cigarettes. It became an everyday part of my life.

The summer from freshman to sophomore year I continued my downfall. Some friends and I would go to the local grocery store and fill up a grocery cart full of food, and on the bottom of the cart we would put a couple cases of beer. We would walk around the store for a few minutes acting like we were still shopping, then we would make our way to the back of the store where there was an emergency exit door that we knew the alarm didn't work. We would grab the beer and haul ass out back and run until we were at a safe distance. Amazingly, we never got caught, but damn I feel bad about doing that.

That same summer after shoplifting some beer, I ended up with two girls, who were a year older, they had their driver's license and a car. My buddy Maxwell was with me. We were sitting in one of the girl's cars drinking beer; the car was parked. There was a pond nearby which Maxwell and one of the girls walked over to. Meanwhile, I asked the girl I was with if I could drive around the parking lot, and she said yes. Not more than thirty seconds after I got behind the wheel, three cop cars with sirens blaring flew into the parking lot. One pulled in front of me and leaped out of his patrol car and signaled me to stop, and being the first time, I have ever been in the driver seat of a car, I accidentally hit the damn gas instead of the brake.

"Holy shit, wrong pedal Brodee," screamed the girl that was with me. I immediately found the brake, and stopped on a dime. The cop dove to the side of the car, I automatically took my hands off the wheel, like I had been in this situation before. He ordered me to get out of the car, I obviously followed his demands, I was scared shitless. My cop had me under control, the other two officers chased Maxwell around the pond. The cops were yelling, drop the beer, I heard Maxwell yell back, noooo, I had to giggle at that.

Maxwell was contained, I was in the back of the patrol car, our parents were called, and on their way. As I sat in the back of the cop car, I asked the officer multiple times if I could go pee, he denied my request. So unfortunately, I couldn't hold it no more, I pissed my pants, but holy crap, it was such a relief. I didn't feel bad because I asked him to pee, and I knew I was going home, so I didn't care. What sucks for him, is that it was July, and the next day was very hot, there was no Febreze back then to cover up the smell of hot piss.

Maxwell's mom made it and took him home, he didn't even receive a citation. My mom showed up on crutches, struggled to get out of her car and hobbled her way toward me and beat me in the leg with her crutch. I couldn't remember why she was on crutches. Either way, I wasn't sure if I should have laughed, or take it seriously. I decided to take it seriously, I felt bad, I had let my parents down and disappointed them. Luckily, the officer let me off with a possession and consumption of alcohol citation, he could have given me a DUI (Driving Under the Influence). It was a quiet, smelly ride home. My parents grounded me, I went to bed, and once again I woke up and the sun was shining. It was my birthday, July 8th, and damnit, since I got in trouble the night before I had to mow the lawn on my birthday. Oh well, I accepted my punishment for being a jackass.

During all my partying and getting in trouble, I always managed to hold a job. Work and sports are always great ways to stay engaged to stay out of trouble. Apparently, I was great at that age of managing school, a job, sports, alcohol and drugs all at once. By all means, I am not proud of those days, but like I said, I can't change the past. I am proud of always going to work, never calling in sick, always finishing my homework, and I even made my bed every morning, but I had this inner devil in me that needed to get high.

There are a hundred stories I could tell about, drugs, drinking, smoking, and being high at Smoky Hill High School, but that's a whole other book. Although those two years in my life are a small percentage of my first forty, every second, minute, hour and day make us who we are.

Hopefully I was starting to grow up, the partying became less, my hours at work became more. I was still smoking an occasional joint; cigarettes and beer were a norm. I also started playing on an intramural basketball league that kept me busy.

Writing about these days is a little uncomfortable for me, there is so much more that happened throughout those two short years, as well as my last two years in high school, but it's hard to talk about. I could write for days, but I have to move on.

Finally, I started accepting who I was, the side effects of further mass destruction within my head from LSD were coming to an end.

Not sure what went on the rest of my sophomore year, it was a blur, but I was aware what happened in the world during that time.

The Los Angeles riots erupted after the beating of Rodney King and the four officers who beat him were acquitted. During the riots, a little over sixty people were killed, one billion dollars in property damage and twelve thousand people were arrested. I remember the news and pictures, LA looked like a war zone, and in some instances it was. As we tried to heal our own wounds here in the United States, the Middle East was getting out of control as well.

Iraq invaded Kuwait, that is when the United States and the UN stepped in and pushed Saddam Hussein and his military all the way back to Baghdad Iraq. George Bush Senior was our current president. The war was named the one hundred hour war, the UN and the United States annihilated the Iraq Army. M1A1 tanks destroyed everything in their path, but it rapidly came to an end. The decision was made not to advance into Baghdad, Saddam Hussein and his Army were spared, for now anyways.

My dad had recently retired from the Air Force, and I remember him saying that he had a possibility of being called back up for the war, luckily, he never was. I never been much of an on the spot emotional person. Therefore, I didn't mention anything to anyone about my dad maybe leaving to war, but deep down inside it bothered me.

We lived out in the economy instead of the Air Force base; and in my opinion no one cared about the military around that time. Maybe the reason why is because nothing had happened since Vietnam and the Cold War with the USSR, so I think the country were naïve to foreign affairs at the time.

All in all, I made it through sophomore year, I was finding myself, my parents were still fighting and getting separated, President Bush and The UN made their point to the world, "Don't mess with Us, or any of our allies", and I was working, going to school and becoming a young adult quicker than I expected.

MATURING

Junior year had begun, my mother left to another state and never returned. My dad and I were forced to move in to an apartment. My brother was already out on his own, it was his first year out of high school. I worked at a pizza joint, and my dad worked at a fast food chicken joint right across the street from the pizza place. The good thing is we always had dinner, either chicken or pizza. Although my dad was retired Air Force, the retirement pay was barely enough to survive on. I had to work to pay for my own habits, and we needed to help each other out.

As far as school, I breezed through my Junior year. I never took advanced classes, just the basics to get my credits, and I also received credits for working.

I still attended parties every now and then with my best friend, I haven't mentioned him much, but we were close. I didn't have a car, in the mornings he would come pick me up for school, and we always had a cigarette on the way to school.

I was doing good, I felt in charge of my life for the first time. I look back now and wish I was more involved in high school, and didn't take it for granted. Maybe I was to focused on being an adult, and forgetting that I was still a teenager who needed more direction. I still had a little demon in me that would talk me into having the occasional beer, smoke, and fun smoke, and that shit demon still had me doing other dumb stuff.

For instance, a few kids I was friends with stopped talking to me due to my alcohol and drug use, which was totally understandable. But, those same kids who defriended me, were now asking me for weed and LSD. It made me laugh, I felt like a veteran of drugs and alcohol, and I was in my recovery stage, and these rookies were just getting started.

I'm not trying to give pointers in any way, shape or form, but when those kids asked, I delivered. I sold them some of the best oregano, and catnip, and the dumb shits actually smoked it and said it was great stuff. It wasn't all oregano and catnip, I left some weed in the bag, probably 30% weed, 35% oregano, and 35% catnip = 100% Aurora, Colorado weed. Obviously, my point being, I ripped them off, and made extra money. One more story about drug dealing, then it's time to move on. Those kids, again asked me for some LSD, they needed five hits, I told them I would have it the next day. That evening, I took an index card and cut five small squares, and then put the squares in a sandwich bag, that recently had one hundred pieces of LSD in it, the reason I mention this is because there might have been some residue left from the hits of LSD. With that being said, I added a couple drops of water to moisten and hopefully mix the leftover LSD with the five pieces of index card. The following day I brought them to school and sold those small, square index cards for five dollars apiece, which was a whole twenty five bucks, but back then, that was a twelve pack of beer, cigarettes, like five gallons of gas, a pizza, movies from an actual movie store, totaling $21.13 and still have $3.87 leftover for two number ones from Taco Bell. The following Monday I asked them how it was, they said amazing. I thought to myself, what the hell, it was just an index card.

After a couple more, times of ripping off jocks with fake drugs, I stopped doing it, I didn't want to have any more involvement with drugs, except for my occasional use.

My senior year quickly approached, I was still kicking butt at the pizza joint.

I was also still playing a lot of basketball, and my three years of high school that were behind me, I had earned enough credits to pretty much make my senior year a walk in the park.

First and second period I had auto class, where we learned the basic mechanics of automobiles, like; oil changes, replacing brakes, tune-ups, tire machine, etc....it was a good class. I also managed to purchase my first vehicle, which was a 1980 Mercury Capri, same as a Mustang only cheaper, I worked on it a lot during those two hours in the morning. Another perk to auto class was if you were late getting to class you just had to buy donuts for the class, and all was forgotten by the teachers, but I was never late. I did enjoy donuts though. My third and final class for the day was a tough one, badminton and swimming. Honestly, it was tough for me, the reason being, that I had acne so bad on my back and chest that I was embarrassed to take my shirt off and go swimming. Fortunately, the school understood and worked with me, I was able to come in by myself during Christmas break and do all the swim strokes to pass the class. Have you ever done the butterfly stroke while your feet touch the bottom of the pool and your arm and head are in motion making it look like you are doing the butterfly stroke? Well that's how I manipulated that stroke, butterfly stroke is hard, but I passed the class with an A.

The time had come, that Christmas break I had finished high school. I had enough credits from those last three classes and credits from on the job training. I manipulated the school and asked them to graduate me a semester early because my dad had plans to move back to Texas, and I was working full time, and supporting myself. They were awesome about the situation, and within a few weeks my diploma was mailed to me, it wasn't real for me until I received it and had my diploma in hand. As I held it, it brought a smile to my face, it was a huge accomplishment for me.

Pushing forward and looking back I realize how grueling high school can be, not for all kids, but for some it can be a life changer. Kids are subject to drinking and drugs, kids are bullied, and made fun of for many different reasons. I wish I could tell some of these kids, that when you are done with high school, none of that bullshit matters. Unfortunately, sometimes these acts result in harming themselves and in extreme situations even suicide.

There are some good kids and friends of mine who lost their lives over making wrong decisions, but knowing if they were still alive to this day, I am sure they would be successful adults. RIP, to all eleven of them, they will never be forgotten. I couldn't imagine the struggle they felt within themselves. If it were drugs that was the cause, sadness, or strictly just teenage bad decision making, I still think of them and how each one could of contributed to life.

No kid should have memories of death and drugs while going through high school. Kids should be remembering homecoming dates, pep rallies, school pride week, prom dates, sports, academic clubs and your high school sweetheart. We shouldn't have to remember the young kids who lost their lives due to drugs, depression or bullying.

I do regret my drug use and partying in high school, but I always try to take bad decision making and turn it into positive thoughts. As crazy as it sounds, drugs made me grow up fast, it taught me that I wanted to live, I wanted to succeed in life, I didn't want to be that lost soul in the darkness the rest of my life.

So what I do is again educate my son, and our child to come and others who struggle with drugs on what not to do. I constantly express the importance of being involved in high school, staying away from the peer pressure, not bullying kids because of their appearance or beliefs. The bottom line is that the kid who got bullied is going to be successful with a great family and house, the kid who had bad acne is going to be a model, the drug addict might work for a rehab center helping addicts, and on the other side, the popular individual with straight A's and a hot girlfriend or boyfriend could end up in prison or strung out. We never know what path everyone will take after those four years of high school, the only path that matters is yours.

There I was, out of high school, my dad was preparing to move to Texas, I had a job I enjoyed at an oil changing place, and although I graduated a semester early I still had friends that I would hang out with, two of them became my lifelong friends. Although I was content with where I was in life, I knew I had to make some decisions about what to do with myself for the next chapter of my life, and sometimes I think fate and God made those decisions for me.

PARTED CLOUDS TO HEAVEN

Sometime my senior year, I can't remember the exact dates, but myself and my best friend (BF) took a road trip down to see my family and grandparents, I couldn't believe his parents let us. My dad was good with it because he was heading down soon anyways. I was seventeen he was sixteen, his parents even let us drive their Honda Accord, the only stipulation was absolutely no smoking in the car. Well, we were teenagers, so you know how that went.

We hit the road, and of course before we even got out of our state BF got a speeding ticket. Actually, we weren't even a hour into the nine hundred mile drive when we got pulled over, but it was a small speeding ticket, so we continued on. We drove straight south into Texas, and holy cow, literally, holy cow, there is not shit but cows from the border of New Mexico and Texas until you get to Amarillo. So, "Amarillo by morning, Amarillo's on my mind", that is a great country song by George Strait, I was singing it a few miles out of Amarillo. BF told me to shut the hell up, hahaha.

Dallas was the next big city, and damn, we are two teenagers that have never done a road trip and when we hit Dallas it was intimidating, and everyone needs to realize we had a map, you know! That big paper thing with different colored lines on it for roads and rivers and such. Exactly, no GPS or cell phones with us, just straight up map reading, and following signs, I think it's called common sense.

45

After nineteen hours of non-stop driving, except for gas and snacks, we made it to my families small town in southern Texas. It was very humid, my friend wasn't used to it, but I have been going down there throughout my childhood.

My grandparents land was one mile back into a thick forest, with several ponds and swamps nearby, it was beautiful, quiet, and filled with wildlife; snakes, spiders, crawdads, mosquitoes, yellowjackets, you know all the nice southern bugs and reptiles. Despite the bad critters, there are beautiful fire flies that begin to flicker at twilight, frogs singing throughout the night, panthers screaming in the deep thicket, and that peaceful country hum. My grandfather had a sign posted on the way to their land that read 'Country Music', referring to the peaceful critters and animals you hear deep in the thick woods. It's an absolutely calming sound, I would close my eyes, listen, and let God's surroundings engulf me.

While we were down there we spent a day in Galveston, on the Gulf Coast. Galveston is a fun coastal town, a lot of history, cruise ships, dolphins jumping in the water and great restaurants. We also visited an alligator farm, which I fell in love with, I love gators, they are extraordinary animals. They had a fourteen foot gator there named Big Al, he had part of his bottom jaw shot off by a shot gun, nonetheless, he was a sweetheart. All in all, it was a good vacation, I also think it was a great confidence builder for us two teenagers to make a trip like that and get home safely. The sad part is, him and I took a polaroid picture (Yes kids, no cell phones), we were wearing snake skin boots, jeans and Body Guard T-shirts, I have searched and searched for that photo and cannot find it, that is one of the last memories I had with my best friend.

Back home, early 1994, the Dallas Cowboys beat the Buffalo Bills in Super Bowl XXVlll, that was the last time Dallas was worth a crap. That same weekend was an emotional weekend for myself, our high school, and community.

The reason being, I had a party at my apartment, lots of kids were there in a small area, but it was a good time. Then a fight happened that changed a lot of people's lives. A friend and I, who I will call Spirit, got into a fight with each other, some punches were thrown, he pistol whipped me on the head twice, my brother and another friend tackled him, and after that, words were exchanged and he left. The rest of the weekend he was calling my house threatening to kill me. My dad and I called the cops. I had friends over that Sunday to watch the Super Bowl, while constantly being on guard. That Monday, a police officer had come to our apartment, my dad walked down the stairs to meet him in the parking lot. As I watched from the balcony the officer raised is hand to his temple and did a shooting motion to the side of his head, I knew right away what had happened. The officer left, my dad came back inside and told me what had happened, I instantly felt sick to my stomach.

Spirit was with two mutual friends of ours, the cops had cornered them in a cul-de-sac, they were in my friends vehicle, apparently on their way to my place, not sure if that was true or not. Nonetheless, Spirit had an altercation with the cops and ended up ending his life by shooting himself.

To this day I do not know what to think about that weekend, we were friends, and then a pointless fight between us ended in tragedy. I blamed myself for years, and I was also not liked by many people because of what happened, I was definitely not welcome at his funeral which I didn't attend, knowing I wasn't welcome. His younger sister did not talk to me for years after his death, but one day I was walking into the grocery store, she was walking out, as we passed each other our eyes met for a brief moment, but we kept walking. Then I hear her call my name, I turned around and we finally spoke after many years, it gave me butterflies, it was a relief, all was forgiven, I needed that from her. Her and I still talk to this day.

A few years before that my family had let Spirit stay at our house for Christmas, not sure why he stayed with us but I didn't question the reasoning, I was just happy he stayed with us. So happy I bought him a Slayer t-shirt for Christmas. He loved it. Needless to say, I wish me and him never got into a fight that Super Bowl weekend.

Spring of '94, my dad was living in Texas, and I had decided to move down there as well, I wanted change, I needed to get out of my current home town. Everything happened so fast, I said goodbye to my best friend. Two of my good friends helped me load a UHAUL trailer with the little possessions I had, and my two cats, we hooked the trailer to one of my friends S10 Blazer and headed south to my families compound in Texas.

The drive down there was fun, we blared Rage Against The Machine and Led Zeppelin, just those two cassette tapes. We had to turn the cassette tape over when one side was done playing, remember that? The cats were nice and calm, it probably was because the truck was clam baked with marijuana smoke, pretty much put Cheech and Chong to shame.

I made it once again to Texas, I shacked up at my Aunts house, which was where I was going to live until I figured life out. I had four sets of Aunts and Uncles, plus my Grandparents who all lived on my Grandparents land. My sister in law would call it the 'Reed Compound'.

My friends stayed for a few days, and can't remember why, but my brother was down there as well, maybe just visiting. Anyway, the guys were all eighteen at the time, I was seventeen, and the drinking age in Louisiana was still eighteen back then. So my brother and those two drove to the border of Louisiana where there were two night clubs right across the Texas line. It wasn't but a twenty minute drive from Sour Lake. To make a long story short, they showed back up to the house after several hours, one of my good friends had a big bandage above his right eye, he had fell off the bar stool and split his head open right above his eye, HAHAHA. They had fun.

Those two headed back to Denver, I had a job lined up at a chicken farm, I began work right away. There were three long rows filled with fifty eight thousand chickens, three to five chickens shoved into a two foot by two foot cage, and they shit eggs day and night. The sad part is, an average of six chickens would die a day, from getting stomped on or from the Texas heat. One of my duties was to walk the long aisles of chickens and pull the dead ones from the cage, and stick them in a unplugged freezer. Once a week I drove them to that alligator farm I mentioned earlier, and the owner of the alligator farm would feed the chickens to the gators. Maintaining a farm like that is hard work, sun up to sun down. When I ate lunch all the flies would munch on my sandwich and chips, I have never seen so many flies in my life, but after while they become your friends. I was beat every day, and when I went home, I didn't want chicken for dinner. My clothes smelled like chicken shit, I had maggots squashed into the bottoms of my boots from having to weld chains together. The chains pushed the chicken crap on a conveyor belt that shot it out into a dump truck, occasionally it missed the truck, so the truck ended up surrounded with chicken poopoo.

Once that truck was filled I waddled my way through two feet deep of chicken feces, and I would climb in the cab of the dump truck, run the windshield wipers in attempt to clear the poo, good enough to see, and then go dump it in piles that were sold for compost.

All in all, I respect farm work, and although its shitty work, the end result is millions of eggs getting cooked for breakfast in American home.

Despite learning a lot about chicken farms, and working my butt off, I had to quit the job. The owner's son ran the place, and he was a back woods redneck dickhead, he treated me like shit, literally. I didn't put up with it for long, and landed a job with my Aunt at the local Dairy Queen. Yes, it crossed my mind what parents and teachers would always say, do you really want to flip burgers the rest of your life? Well at the time heck yeah I did. In my opinion every job is respectful, I don't care if its flipping burgers, being a janitor, or bagging groceries, I have always taken pride in where I worked. Not to mention, I made one hell of a burger, Dairy Queen burgers are amazing.

Life wasn't so bad, I was working, making a little money, and I would keep in touch with my best friend on a regular basis, he seemed like he was doing well.

On my days off I would help around the Reed Compound, mostly helping my grandparents out. They had a lot of land, so I used the riding lawn mower to mow the lawn. Something happened one day when I was mowing, I calmly came to a brief stop, I stared into the clouds, the clouds parted leaving a clear path into Heaven, it looked like a blue tunnel, it was beautiful, the dark blue sky, surrounded by white puffy clouds. After squinting up for a few seconds I continued to mow, not thinking much of what just took place. I went and parked the mower under an old shed my grandfather had built by hand in the forties. I finished the day with a good home cooked southern meal; okra, sweet corn, corn bread, black eyed peas, brisket, and a tall glass of milk. I remember that meal vividly. After dinner I retired to bed.

The following morning I woke to roosters singing to the sunrise, the smell of biscuits and bacon, my aunt yelling at my cousins to get their asses up, while she smoked on the porch in her long country night gown. Mid-morning had come, I was outside by the pond, my aunt yelled for me, her voice carried out in the country. A dead man could have heard her. I walked over to see what she wanted.

She said to me "your Grandma didn't want me to tell you this, but you need to know, I just got a phone call from BF's mom. He had passed away." I fucking lost it, tears rushed down my face. I was numb. I couldn't believe it. It wasn't real. My grandmother didn't want me to know, because she knew I would go back home, and sure enough she was right. I knew there was symbolism to the clouds parting the day before, it all made sense, it was BF going to heaven.

I started looking for a way back to my old town. My family had no money, and I had very little myself, luckily the Greyhound bus line only charged twenty nine dollars one way. I was able to afford that, I packed a small suitcase, some cheese and crackers, and headed back home. Unfortunately, I was going to miss his funeral, it had taken me a few days to come up with money and a way back, but BF's family and the funeral home agreed to have him available for me to spend time with him when I returned.

The day I got home, my friend picked me up from the bus station, he brought me to an area nearby BF's parents' house. I wanted to walk and clear my head, and go over in my mind how it was going to be emotionally when I made it to their house. No words in the world can help any parent when they experience the loss of a child. I just had to do it, all I could do is be there with them and grieve together. As I walked up the front porch, the door was wide open, a lot of family members and friends were scattered throughout the house. I hugged BF's mom, dad and sister. No words were exchanged, just tears. We all went down to his room and sobbed for what seemed like hours. BF's dad held me and I held him. There is no worse feeling in the world than a soul being ripped away from your heart. We all needed each other. After a long afternoon, and a night of no sleep, a mutual friend took me to see BF.

When we arrived a lady met me at the funeral home front door. She escorted me in. I stood at the end of the aisle, there were maybe twenty rows of benches on each side of the aisle, and at the end of the aisle rested BF. He was dressed in a nice suit, his hair perfect like always, he was a very handsome kid. It was just me and him, I slowly walked down to his casket, he was pale, but I had a strong feeling inside of me it was just a body, his spirit and soul were already in heaven. I couldn't accept that it was him, I screamed out a loud NOOOOOO, and left the funeral home.

Damn, I miss him. He used to tell me his passion was to fly a jet for the Air Force, I used to get jealous of him because he could get any girl he wanted, not only because of his looks, but because of his awesome attitude. Squirrels use to climb on his shoulders in his front yard, they trusted him. He loved snakes and reptiles, we didn't agree on snakes. I would have to go snake hunting with him east of Denver, the whole time I was thinking to myself fuck snakes, I hope we don't see any, HAHA, but he was my friend, and I loved hanging out with him. He was gone, I couldn't eat or sleep for weeks. His parents let me stay at their house because I had nowhere else to go. I slept in his room, it was weird at first because he died in there, but after a few days I would talk to him. Sometimes I swear the stereo would all the sudden turn on, or lights would flicker, I just knew he was there with me.

The night of his death neighbors said they remember seeing him pulling into the garage listening to the soundtrack from the movie *The Crow*. The next morning his mom went to wake him up, the door was shut to his bedroom. She knocked and there was no answer. She opened the door, he was hanging from a noose that he used for his pet lizard, it was hooked to a weight machine, his knees barely off the ground. For the life of me I cannot imagine what she goes through, my heart goes out to her every day of my life. His death was ruled a suicide, I don't believe that to this day.

Time always continues to tick, with all the heart ache, drama, and even love, and happiness, life continues.

SHORTY MAXWELL

I slept in BF's room for a few months. I started back up at Grease Monkey changing oil, and other small services on cars, I purchased a 1977 Volkswagen bug for five hundred dollars, and if you can get a bug running it will never quit, it was a reliable vehicle.

Eventually, I told myself I had to get out of BF's parents' house and live on my own. I searched around in the newspaper (Yes kids, not craigslist or Facebook), for a place to live, and gratefully a buddy I worked with had an old friend that needed a roommate.

The house was located in a bad part of the big city. It was a ranch style home, very small, two bedroom, the kitchen, living room and bathroom all on the same floor. Cigarette smoke lingered throughout the home, but I was good with it since I smoked. The carpet looked to be the original carpet that came with the house, a shaggy brown color, he had a mismatched couch and recliner. I can't remember the old man's name, but needless to say I will never forget what he did for me.

The first night I stayed there, he showed me my room, just big enough to fit a single bed and a small dresser. The refrigerator was an old school retro style, with the big heavy door handles. It could have probably survived a nuclear blast. Inside it had butter, half a loaf a bread and a bottle of Skol Vodka. Next was the bath tub, no shower, just a simple stand alone, cast iron bath tub, that was stained from years of neglect. I couldn't complain about anything, I was happy to have a roof over my head, and I was going to make it work until I figured out what I wanted to do with my life.

First things first, I went to the store and spent my last twenty dollars on sandwich stuff, the biggest bottle of 409, scrub pads, and ajax, and I went to town on that bath tub. It looked brand new when I was done with it. The old man was very thankful, and not to be mean, but I took a bath before he did, and then of course cleaned it before every use.

I continued to work hard throughout the summer at the oil change shop. I spent a lot of time with Maxwell and BF's family, I also joined a gym, which helps with everyday life. It's good to get a workout in, deal with some of the stress in life, and to offset the drinking, smoking, and fast food consumption. After all, you should balance everything.

As for now I was somewhat content with my life, I just wasn't going anywhere, but I had a job, a place to live, and a car. Along with all that, the country had a lot going on, both good and bad.

The good stuff first, *The Lion King* and *Forest Gump* were both released that summer of '94, and they are still popular to this day, I have watched them time and time again. Sony PlayStation came out as well, I was never much of a gamer, so didn't care to much for it. *Friends*, the TV show aired for the first time, my son is currently watching all the episodes, it will be around for a long time, love you Jennifer Aniston. Lastly, Justin Bieber was born in 1994.

Now, the bad entertainment stuff that took place during 1994. During a practice for the US Women's Championship for figure skating, and which would also decide who qualifies for the Olympics, Nancy Kerrigan was struck in the leg with a Baton, causing swelling and bruising. The attacker was identified as now ex-husband of figure skater Tonya Harding. This goes down as one of the biggest sports scandals ever. Despite the injury, Nancy Kerrigan went on to receive silver the following day, Tonya Harding finished in eighth place. To this day Tonya Harding denies any involvement in the attack, hmmmm. We will just leave it at that.

Then there was OJ Simpson, former NFL football player/actor. He was accused for the deaths of his ex-wife Nicole Brown and her friend Ron Goldman. The murders took place June of '94 and the most watched trial of all time began January of '95, which led to his acquittal.

If the glove doesn't fit, you must acquit. In a sarcastic way, I believe that famous phrase is used to this day to symbolize innocence. It was the phrase used to help in judgement of the OJ Simpson trial. Although he was found innocent, karma later caught up with him in life and he spent time in prison for other crimes.

Sadly, in the music world, Kurt Cobain from Nirvana took his own life, but on the other hand Justin Bieber was born, it might be a coincidence, one great performer dies, and another is born. But I am not saying Justin Bieber comes close to the music Nirvana made, I am just saying Justin Bieber is a great performer.

Remember when I talked about Dimples? That is the girl I went to see *Forest Gump* with that summer of '94. Unfortunately, we were with several other people so it wasn't a date, matter of fact she didn't even talk to me. Regardless, it was a great movie.

Christmas of '94 came around, my brother was living in town, and although we didn't talk much, we hung out Christmas day and went to a movie. We saw *Tombstone*, another great movie. "I will be your Huckleberry", Doc Holidays famous line.

That was the last time I hung out with my brother, not that we disliked each other or anything like that, life just took us in different paths.

Now it was time to get real, I had to make something of my life, and who better to decide that with me was Maxwell. We were sitting in his room at his mother's house having beer and talking life, we were feeling good. Smoking and drinking, and Maxwell says to me, you wanna go to the Army recruiter tomorrow. Well that shit never crossed my mind, but hell yes, I was all for it, I mean what did I have to lose.

That next day we went to the recruiter, we were both eighteen, mature young drinking, smoking adults. As we walked inside the recruiter office there were all four branches of military posted on the wall, and along the hallway with offices on each side, the hallway was filled with posters of jets for the Air Force, battle ships for the Navy, mud and guns for the Marines, and tanks for the Army. Of course, all the recruiters from each branch would yell at you as you were in the hallway. The Air Force recruiter in a sophisticated voice would say, Join the Air Force, its where all the smart kids go, and we sleep in hotels and eat great food. Well everything sounded good, except I wasn't that bright. The Marine would yell in a deep manly voice, come join the Marines, we are first in battle, and mean as hell, OORAH, KILL KILL KILL. Yeah no thanks. Then there is the Navy guy, with a soft little voice, come float with the Navy, we spend weeks at a time at sea, with hundreds of great seamen. Again, no thanks. Finally, the Army, a little black man wired like a chihuahua on crack, he said, you two look like future Soldier, come in my office and let me show you your future. His name was Sergeant First Class (SFC) Shorty. He was an awesome guy, and for the next few months he helped in preparing me for a huge life change. Granted he had to work his ass off to get several waivers for me to get accepted into the Army. I had two possession and consumption tickets for alcohol, an assault and battery ticket, because a buddy and I got in a fight with some kids throwing gang signs at us, and lastly a few minor traffic offenses. SFC Shorty had his hands full, not to mention, Maxwell was no saint either.

While SFC Shorty was working his magic to get myself and Maxwell into the Army, my living with the old man was coming to an end. I couldn't take the nastiness anymore. I would come home from work and he would have already downed a bottle of vodka, he would stumble around the house wearing only torn up underwear, talking gibberish, and occasionally glancing at me in confusion like he didn't understand who I was or why I was there. I felt bad for the old man, he was lonely, an alcoholic, and lived in the dark, but I was also scared for myself. I didn't feel comfortable living there anymore. The very next morning, I woke up, got ready for work, quietly loaded my belongings into my bug, and went to work. I never spoke to him or went back to that house again.

It was the end of January 1995, still winter out, I slept in my bug for a few nights until I got paid, then I would go re-group at a hotel room for the night. I did this for about a month, then luckily my brother got an apartment and I went to stay on his couch.

SFC Shorty called me once again, he drove me down to MEPS (Military Entrance Processing Station) in Denver. I passed my physical and got the all clear to go. SFC Shorty told me with the scores I had from taking the Army Services Vocational Aptitude Battery (ASVAB), it's a multiple-choice test, I had two choices on what I could do in the Army. Infantry or Tanker. Yes, I scored very low, duuhhhh, so naturally my choices were combat arms. Walking all over with the Infantry didn't sound exciting, then he showed me videos of the M1A1 Abrams Tank, and I was sold, it looked awesome, I didn't have to walk with the Infantry, I would get to ride in the most powerful land machine known to man.

March 28th, 1995, SFC Shorty picked me up in a Ford Taurus that had US Government plates on it, he took me to the airport to fly out to basic training. I shook his hand, and he said good luck Soldier.

SMOKE 'EM IF YA GOT 'EM

Eighteen years old, and headed to the Army, I was picked up at the airport by a blue school bus, and several guys in Army uniform. I thought they would be yelling already, but these were logistic guys, the yelling and ass chewing's came later. I remember the building they took all the new recruits too, but I can't remember what was going through my head, I actually just think for the first time in my short eighteen years on this planet I was worry free, and was ready to start this new chapter of my life.

In my small bag I brought, I had three packs of Marlboro's, I was smoking like a chimney, because I knew the time was coming when I wasn't going to be able to smoke. This wasn't the Vietnam era, this was 1995, nicotine wasn't aloud at basic training.

Chain smoking outside. A loud voice yelled, smoke 'em if you got 'em. We were loading the bus again to head to the lovely Ft. Knox Kentucky, home of the M1A1 Abrams tank. I threw half a cigarette away, and lit another, to get a full fix in. We started loading the bus. All contraband, cigarettes, lighters, and alcohol were to be turned in before loading the bus, and all they said was, please let us catch you with some shit when we get to post. With that being said, I threw all my pack of smokes, and lighters in the contraband can and got on the bus. That was it for smoking for the time being, but it didn't bother me, because when we arrived at Ft. Knox I didn't have time to think about smoking.

It was late at night, the Sergeants assigned all the new recruits bunks for the night in Army barracks with about twenty people to a bay. The following morning we were woken by calm voices, and that was the last time those calm voices were heard for the next ninety days.

We were instructed to gather in the parking lot, and we did, literally a gathering. Then from around the red brick building all of us slept in, came six, straight faced, yelling assholes. They were in green camouflage uniforms, black boots that looked like glass because of the shine they put on the boots, and these guys were different from the rest of the Army men I have encountered from the airport to now. These guys had on olive drab colored hats, with a rim around it, basically a high crown cowboy hat, but it was intimidating. Not sure if it was the hat that was intimidating or the crazy ass wearing it. Sure enough, I figured it out, those were Drill Sergeants. They quickly and aggressively told us to line up in columns and rows.

Picture in your head, four rows deep, and in each row, thirty different Americans from every part of the country. The Idaho boy that was pale as snow, the LA kid wearing a dark blue Dodgers cap, a Texas boy waddling in his shit kickers, and a Virginia boy looking like he joined the Army just for free dental. Then there was me, scared, young and lonely, but somehow found it within myself to get motivated, and push through the next thirteen weeks of hell and give it my all, and why not? I had nothing else to do.

Week one at basic training, was called reception week. They taught us the basics of marching, and staying in a formation. The first place they marched us to was the barber. I had thick, shoulder length hair that was gone in less than two minutes, they shaved us bald, and when all the heads were shaved, I thought to myself, white, Asian, black, Hispanic, fat, skinny, or whatever, we all had shaved heads, we were all equal.

Next the Drill Sergeants sat us down in a room, and handed out blank check books to everyone with two hundred dollars in a personal checking account they set up for us. I felt like I hit the lottery, but then they marched us to a shoppette where running shoes, hygiene products, Army brown towels and rags, Army brown underwear, or white boxers were sold. Needless to say, I spent close to my two hundred dollars and couldn't even buy a snickers bar.

That first week wasn't bad at all, I called Maxwell and told him it was kind of cool, he left for basic training a couple weeks after me, so he was still home in Colorado. That first week was just a tease, because exactly a week after I had been there, shit hit the fan.

Every bald headed recruit formed up in the parking lot, it was early morning,. I wasn't used to the cold wetness of the south, it was bone chilling standing out there, but I had to man up, I had to find motivation within myself, and luckily I had no choice, motivation found me.

Some new Drill Sergeants(SGT's) showed up, they began to pick recruits out, like a sports draft. Some of the comments from Drill SGT's were; I will take this Pillsbury boy, and whoop his fat ass into shape, or, you think you are gangsta bitch?, I will take this ghetto fuck. How about, give me that little white nerd with glasses, I will make him a killing machine, and one more, this was the best, he a pretty motherfucker, can't wait to meet his mom. Yep, there were no filters from Drill SGT's mouth's, just the truth.

I was drafted by Drill SGT Bulldog. He was short, bull dog shaped, square head, and smelled like cigarettes, my other Drill SGT was a six foot six-inch tall black guy. He would lick his lips, and roll his tongue when he was about to tear your ass up, but he never cursed, and he actually had that calm, scary vibe to him. I respected him greatly, his name was Drill SGT Soul, turns out he was a very religious man, I saw him as a great leader as well.

I was officially in Charlie Company 2/13 Armor unit, basic training at Fort Knox, Kentucky. The two Drill Sergeants silently marched us about a mile to our barracks, home for the next thirteen weeks, they calmly said, find a bunk, and we will see you bright and early, 0430.

I found a bunk, I had to sleep on the top bunk, the guy below me was one of the older recruits, he was thirty two, he was a great guy, and someone in our platoon everyone could look up to, we called him Grandpa.

Although I was lacking nicotine, alcohol, and freedom, I slept like a baby on that bunk. I was stress free. I was in a place where I had a home, three meals a day, and no worries about where I was going in life.

That next morning I didn't need an alarm, holy shit, the Drill SGT's came in yelling and pounding on things to get the hell up, and we had two minutes to be downstairs. I made it down on time, some recruits didn't, and man, did they pay for it. When they finally made it downstairs out to the front of the barracks, the Drill SGT's smoked the shit out of them (smoked the shit out of them means performing any exercise imaginable until muscle failure was reached). That was an eye opener for me, I thought to myself, just be where you are supposed to be at the right time, in the right uniform, do what your told, and have motivation.

As the days and weeks went by, it became really good training. I was pumped. I learned how to shoot weapons, throw hand grenades, use radio's, and a lot of other cool Army stuff, as well as getting in shape. Summer began, it became hot and humid every day, and we always started every morning with physical training. Sundays we were allowed to use the phone and make a five minute call from a phone booth, and since no one had quarters you had to make collect calls home, or to a girlfriend, and you just hoped they would accept the collect call. It was almost like calling from prison.

Besides the hurry up and eat, which the food was bland anyways, or the yelling from the Drill SGT's, I had some great memories of those weeks.

My favorite memory was when we were all doing a land navigation course and my team which consisted of two other guys one named Private Bubba, and the other Private Cali. Bubba was a heavy set tall black kid, that had a huge bottom lip and thick bottle cap glasses, we actually called him Bubba from *Forest Gump*. The other Private was Cali from LA, everyone thought he was Mexican, but he was actually Japanese. He was short, skinny and moved around like a mouse, so we nicknamed him house mouse. When we approached our first checkpoint the Drill SGT caught me with my hands in my pocket, which was frowned upon heavily.

He yelled, "private fucking Reed, are your hands cold?"

"No Drill SGT." I yelled back.

"Well since you are playing pocket pool, I want you to go find the smallest rock in that rock pile over there and bring it to me." I jogged over to the rock pile that was nearby, and I searched for the smallest one, but my smart ass cocky self, decided to pick one of the biggest rocks in the pile.

He said, "are you sure you want that one"?

"Fuuuucckkk yeessss Drill SGT." I yelled trying to catch my breath. He smiled and pulled out a sharpie and drew a smiley face on it, and he told me he was going to call the other Drill SGT at the next checkpoint to let him know I am bringing him a present, and that present better make it there. So there I was off to the next check point, that was about a mile and a half away, but carrying a sixty pound rock it seemed ten miles. Luckily, Bubba and Cali helped me with that damn rock. We actually grabbed two branches about five feet long, and we took my poncho and wrapped it around the branches to make a stretcher and put the rock on the stretcher. We decided to name the rock Stoney.

After rolling hills, thick forest, humid-hot weather and thousands of mosquitos and spiders we made it to the next checkpoint with Stoney, and the Drill SGT smirked and calmly said, "what the fuck is that?"

I explained what happened at the previous checkpoint, he laughed and said get rid of that damn rock, and ohhh man, we were happy to toss it. Apparently the Drill SGT at the first checkpoint NEVER EVEN CALLED HIS DRILL SGT BUDDY, I could have left damn Stoney in the forest somewhere, yeah he got me good. From then on I never put my hands in my pockets while I was in uniform.

After finishing a dreaded day of land navigation, everyone was exhausted, dehydrated, hungry and stinky as shit, so what better to do, than go be a good human and give a pint of blood. It was a voluntold blood draw, so you really had no choice. There is a lot of voluntold stuff to do in the Army. But, since I recently had a fresh tattoo I was exempt from doing so.

I became the nurses little helper boy. Of course, being a good leader he was, one of the Drill SGT's went first, and as soon as he laid down he called me over.

"Private Reed, get your ass over here." I shuffled quickly next to his gurney. He spoke again in his loud, forceful voice, "so you are one of those bad ass kids who needs tattoos to think he is a bad ass."

I replied, "no Drill SGT, I am a bad ass regardless."

"Oh is that so Private? Well let's see how bad ass you are." He said "come closer Private." My heart was pounding, sweat trickled down my forehead, as I inched closer and got within reach, BAMMMM, the son-of-a-bitch grabbed my balls.

He calmly says, "let's see how bad ass you are, when the nurse puts the needle in my arm, if it hurts one tiny bit, I going to rip your balls off."

A mumble came out of my mouth, "ye-sss Drill SGT." I can hear laughter all around me from other Soldier. I stood there looking at the nurse with a smirk on her face, barely poking the other arm of the Drill Sgt, and asking, did that hurt? She was playing along. Finally, the Drill SGT and I were staring each other down, she swiftly poked him, his hands released my balls.

"You are lucky I love pain Private, now get out of my face," as he grinned. I never been so relieved in my life, all night in the barracks it gave us Soldier something to laugh at.

It was getting toward the end of basic training, I had learned a lot about myself, and what I was capable of. I also learned that people from all over our great country, black, white, Asian, Mexican, and many others, can get together, survive, rely, and live with each other through the worst of times.

Our last week in basic training was called 'Hell Week'. We road marched in the rain for a week, sleeping on the ground, eating rain drenched Army food, but I loved it, I felt like a warrior. Those Drill SGT's were not going to bring me, or any of my brothers down, we were ready for whatever they threw at us.

It was a rough week, twenty hour days, little food to eat, bad weather, soaked feet, blisters, chafing, you name it, we were beat. But the last night of Hell Week was there finally. Drill SGT's sent us through an obstacle course where bombs were going off next to our heads while we low crawled through the mud. Heart pounding, scared as hell, barbed wire all around, and to top it off a Drill SGT was shooting a 50 Caliber Machine Gun with real ammo in it, so if you were to stand up and jump, you might get shot. It took about an hour for each Soldier to get through, but we all made it, and at the end we celebrated, we were done, we just accomplished Army Basic Training, Combat Arms, Tankers, I was a M1A1 Tanker, an elite crew member of the most powerful machine in the world. I was proud. I needed this brotherhood, and the Army, I belonged to something, I will forever love my brothers I have met throughout my twenty two years in the military.

Graduation day. One day before my nineteenth birthday, July 7th,1995, Ft Knox Kentucky, wearing a slick Army Green Dress Uniform, marching to the parade field, Drill SGT Soul sang cadence, he had a deep voice that made goose bumps appear on one's body, butterflies fluttered in Soldier guts, and pride of a great Nation consumed our minds as we marched and sang loud and proud "The Army Colors".

The Army Colors
The Colors are blue...
To show the world
That we are true...
The Army Colors
The Colors are white...
To show the world
That we will fight...
The Army Colors
The Colors are red...
To show the world
The blood we've shed...
The Army Colors
The Colors are gold...
To show the world
That we are bold...
The Army Colors
The Colors are green...
To show the world
That we are mean...

I graduated from Basic Training. I was proud of myself, and what was the first thing I did? I went and bought a pack of Marlboros, and damn, I not going to lie, it was the best smoke I ever had. I shouldn't promote cigarettes, but the way I saw it, I was eighteen, I just finished thirteen weeks of bad ass training, my tour of duty was in Germany, I was alive, I felt great about myself.

Back home for two weeks, I stayed with BF's mom and dad. For those two weeks, I didn't do much but rest and get caught up on current affairs. I finally had a chance to read about and pray for the families of the Oklahoma City bombing. April 19th, 1995, the piece of shit Timothy

McVeigh and Terry Nichols car bombed Murrah Federal Building in downtown Oklahoma City killing one hundre seventy one, including children and injuring more than six hundred eighty bystanders. It was the biggest domestic terrorist attack in the history of the United States. That cowardly act still affects families and friends to this day. It's sad to say that gutless similar acts like the bombing still take place, probably more now than ever.

In other news, in 1995; Michael Jordan, The best basketball player ever returned from retirement, North America's largest airport opened, Denver International Airport, Christopher Reeve/Superman was paralyzed after he was thrown from his horse, Ebay went live, Operation Desert FOS officially ended, and to top it all off and end on a happy note, Toy Story opened in theatres, the first ever full-length CGI movie.

Then the day came, I was off to a foreign land.

GUTEN TAG TANKER

Not sure who took me to the airport the day I left home to fly to Germany. My only possessions were two Army green duffle bags filled with Army Uniforms and a few civilian clothes. I had no ties to home except for BF's family. My family had all moved away, but I still called it home, I guess I had to be from somewhere.

I boarded an airplane, the name of the airline was Lufthansa, they are an international airline company, and dang it was an enormous plane. They had stairs going to a second floor where you were allowed to smoke cigarettes and have drinks, not sure if it were because it was an international flight that they let passengers smoke, but I wasn't complaining. First stop was Chicago O'Hare airport, had a few hour layover, and then off to Germany.

I landed in Frankfurt Germany, fifteen hours after I left Colorado, it was like traveling through a time machine, I was so jet lagged, I have never felt that way before, I was confused. I exited the plane and sure enough people were allowed to smoke inside the airport, I was already loving Germany and Europe. I couldn't read a damn thing in the airport, but with a little common sense, I headed to baggage claim. There were Soldier there to direct all new military personnel coming to Germany. That was a relief, because I was young, dumb and….. well you know the rest. After gathering my duffle bags, I spent the next few hours in a reception area waiting on my military orders, and after hours of waiting I finally received orders to my post in Southeast Bavaria, Germany. I was ready to get there and get some sleep.

I faintly remember driving on the bus to post, I was in such a daze. To this day I can still hear BMW's, Mercedes, and other German cars zooming past the bus at a high rate of speed, it sounded like I was on a Indy race car track. My head was leaned up to the side window of my bus seat, my eyes periodically opening, to see nothing but forest, and old brick houses, with cobble stone streets.

Numerous times throughout the drive we passed a Autobahn sign that read 'Ausfahrt', I thought to my tired brain, damn Ausfahrt must be a big town in Germany. There is a sign on every exit pointing to Ausfahrt. When we arrived, the bus driver opened the bottom doors to the bus, and the five Soldier I rode with grabbed our duffle bags, as we stood there and waited on our ride in silence.

I asked the group, "did ya'll keep seeing that sign that said something like Ass Fart? That must be a big town." They all started laughing uncontrollably.

One of the Soldier replied, "Ausfahrt (Ass Fart) means exit in German." Well I felt like a dumbass, but we all laughed and it broke the ice.

I spent a week getting checked into post, I actually met up with a guy I went to basic with at Ft. Knox. His name was Chadwick, he was a thirty year old from the swamps of Louisiana. He was a short guy, and looked older than his age, I could tell he had traveled a rough road, and at the time, since I was nineteen, and he was thirty it seemed like he was old as dirt. Despite the age difference, we connected well and hung out for the week touring the post. We found two night clubs right off of post, so guess where we were every night? Hell yes!!! I in Germany sitting at a bar drinking beer, didn't even get asked for my ID. I felt like an adult, life was good, and the German beer knocked me on my ass. I was used to drinking Keystone, Busch or Olympia, whose slogan was, "It's the Water". Needless to say, it was definitely a culture change. We also made it to a small town that bordered post. I fell in love with the cobble stone roads, cathedral's in the village, and century old cottages that line the small streets, the thick forest all around, and century old pubs, that once inside felt like you took a step back in time four hundred years. Germany is an absolutely beautiful country.

As far as the actual post, it was just as nice. There was a German Cantina that served incredible wiener schnitzel, bratwurst, sauerkraut, and many other traditional German foods, and every meal came with pommes frittes (french fries in German). If you weren't tasting German food, every military installation had a Burger King, Anthony's Pizza, a sandwich shop of some sort, and Baskin Robins ice cream. Nothing like a Whopper with Cheese to cure a hangover. ☺ Most of the buildings on post look the same, light brown brick, the Stars and Stripes and Guidons (military flag) representing Tank and Infantry Battalions, flew in front of Headquarters buildings. The landscape kept up extremely well, trees all around, K-12 schools for military families, a movie theatre, and everything the little community needs to survive. The neighborhood where married families and officers lived was quiet and clean, all of this magical land made up half the post.

The other half of post consisted of rows of barracks, filled with young, single, combat arms Soldier ready to kill, party, fight, party some more, than go kill the enemy, then maybe fight and party at the same time. Not only were they the greatest warriors in the world, but they also operated two of the most powerful land fighting machines, the M1A1 Abrams Tank, and the Bradley Fighting Vehicle. I was finally assigned to 2-37 Armor Battalion, I became part of the most powerful brotherhood in the world, Tanker.

I made it to my company's barracks, the bottom floor was the Commanders and First Sergeants (1SG) offices. Across the hall was all the Platoon Sergeants (PLT SGT's) and Lieutenants (LT's/many different names), down the hall from there was a day room with a TV, pool tables and couches. The last two rooms were the arms room, where all weapons were locked up, and SGT Durham's supply room, that resembled a smoked filled bar, but he was the best damn supply SGT I have ever had. The next four floors housed all single Soldier from ranks of Private to Staff Sergeant.

I specifically remember arriving to my barracks on a Sunday, there weren't any Soldier around but I had a Sergeant from staff duty who gave me keys to my room, I was on the top floor. I grabbed my heavy duffle bags and looked around for signs pointing to an elevator, I didn't see any, so I asked the SGT where it was, and he says, ohhh the elevator, yes! Follow me. We walked to the end of the hallway and he pointed up the stairs, there is your elevator Private, Hahaha, he laughed and then ran out the door like he was in a hurry to get off work.

I took a deep breath in, and hauled my two duffle bags up eight flights of cold, hard, stairs. Once at the top, I stood for a few seconds until my breathing returned to normal, not only was I winded from the stairs, but also short of breath due to nerves. Slowly I gathered myself and opened the two steel doors to the hallway. I began to walk down the hall rotating my head side to side looking for my room number. A couple of the doors were propped opened, I passed the first room that was open, Guns n Roses was playing at a low level, Coors Lite beer cans were littered throughout the floor, and cigarettes butts pouring out of one of the cans. The next open room had Snoop Dogg on the stereo playing "Gin and Juice", and the smell of incense mixed with swisher sweets cigars tunneled out the door.

I located my room and made my way inside. Someone was already inside and claimed a bunk, his name was Private Messy Smurf, I went to basic training with him at Ft Knox as well. That was a relief that we were both brand spanking new to A Co 2-37 Armor, Avengers.

Private Messy Smurf was a taller kid, with a Goofy The Dog looking head and face. He had a certain sense of humor to him that would piss you off, but at the same time make you laugh. He had his half of the room already in disarray. I remember him being messy at basic training, I guess he was absent the day the Drill SGT's went through our belongings and threw them everywhere, telling us to have our area organized and spotless every day.

We greeted each other, and I began to unpack my bags, while making small talk with Messy Smurf.

"Kind of quiet out in the hallway." I said.

"Yeah, I heard the majority of the company was at a training placed called Hohenfels, they are supposed to be back at the end of the week," Messy Smurf replied.

I finished putting away all my uniforms and clothes and neatly placed some pictures of myself and a couple of my close friends on my desk. It was getting late, and after a week I still wasn't on track with the time change. I laid in my bunk, half asleep and a loud knock came at the door. Messy Smurf answered it. A guy in a Megadeath tank top and camouflage cargo shorts was at the door. He simply asked if I was in the room and of course Messy Smurf replied yep.

"Okay good, 0615 in the parking lot, uniform is PT's (physical fitness uniform)."

"Did you hear that Reed?"

"Sure did." I replied.

With that being said, I went to plug in my alarm clock that I brought from the states and quickly realized the plug didn't match. Europe runs off 220V, luckily Messy Smurf had a converter I could plug into and make it work. If he didn't I probably would have stayed up all night just so I didn't miss the 0615 formation.

Finally, I woke up feeling rested and normal after a week of jetlag. I made my way down the stairs to formation, I was always early, I've been like that my whole life, sometimes the habit of being early sucks. Nonetheless, I was there on time, due to most of the company being gone, there were only about ten of us in formation. We stretched and went on a three mile run. On our return, Messy Smurf and I were paired up with two Soldier that have been in A Co for a year or so, they were to get us familiarized with the post, assign us to a platoon and take care of some of the other administrative tasks. So the first week was relaxing.

That Friday arrived, the first week was finished. Messy Smurf and I were released until Monday. We walked to the shoppette, approximately five minutes from the barracks to buy some goodies. We both stocked up on cigarettes, a carton of Marlboros was a whopping eleven dollars, and I also stocked up on two cases of Coors Lite, which came to eighteen dollars for both cases. Not too bad considering the fifty five dollars it costs for a carton of smokes now days and twenty five dollars for a case of beer.

Back at the room, I quickly cracked a beer and laid sideways on my bunk, I looked as my side of the room, that was kept neat, and then I looked at Messy Smurfs side and said after swallowing a sip of beer, your shit is nasty.

Clothes were scattered around his bunk on the floor, his covers looked like two dogs wrestled in them all day, and he actually started smelling like BO.

"Well, I thought we got room service," Messy Smurf said with a grin.

"Well room service isn't going to clean your stinky ass, and you know damn well we don't get room service jackass."

We both chuckled, but he still never cleaned his crap up, he just a natural slob, but a funny slob.

Six beers into my two cases, I could hear voices coming up the stairs. As the voices got closer it sounded like a herd of elephants were making their way to the top floor. It was all of A Co back from training. You could hear it in their voices, they were pumped to be back, they were excited for the weekend. One of the Soldier yelled down the hallway, "I'm changing and going to Nuremberg, getting the fuck out of here."

I overheard another Soldier say, "I heard we got some new privates in."

Simultaneously, I got nervous and excited, I just wanted to meet all the Soldier in the company and get it over with.

After a few minutes of them discussing plans for the weekend, the hallways were cleared, but you could hear music from each room; country in one, rap in another, heavy metal slamming in some ex-stoners room. Then there was the Ace of Base in between all the music, I thought to myself, that Soldier must have his German girlfriend already in his room listening to Ace of Base.

About an hour went by, a twelve pack down, Messy Smurf laying in his bed on top of unfolded clothes, and all of the sudden we were bombarded with four guys from the company questioning us on stuff like where we are from, age...blah blah blah. After getting interrogated, SPC Steele spoke.

"Well if you privates are going to be in this company you have buy beer for everyone." I reached down on the side of my bunk and grabbed a case of beer.

"Drink up." I said with confidence.

That night was a success, I had beers with several Soldier in the company, we drank until early morning, I fit in just fine. The following day I was invited to Nuremberg, Germany.

I woke up around eleven, I was feeling a little rough, but the magic cure for my slight hangover was a whopper with cheese.

Back at the barracks, walking down the hallway to my room, an enormous black guy, that look like present day 50 cent on steroids, came my direction. We got about four feet from each other and he flexes up his gigantic arms and yells at me, "you call me a nigga?"

My reaction was Nooooooooo, fuck Nooooo, I would never say that!!!!!!, as I lunged against the brick wall in the fetal position. His name was SPC HMF from Florida. He was one big ass dude.

He smiled and laughed, "I'm just fucking with you Reed, welcome to A Co." We became good friends, he was a great guy, I still talk to him to this day, he still a big ass dude.

I made it to my room, and had to change underwear because of the incident I just encountered. Messy Smurf was gone for the weekend, so it was nice to have the room to myself. I kicked all his clothes to his side of the room, turned on some music and cracked a beer. Then the time came to head to Nuremberg.

There were four of us, myself and SGT from the Phillipines, who I could only pick out a few words in his sentences, but he laughed every time he stopped talking, so I went along with him and laughed as well. The other two were from Lousiana and another SGT that was skinny and dressed like Genuine Dy Crocket, he was white as rice, but claimed to be Native American. We all barely knew each other, but it didn't matter, we automatically bonded because we all wore the US Army uniform, we were ready to sight see and have some fun.

We took a taxi to the train station just outside of post. All taxis are Mercedes Benz, which I thought was pretty cool. If I remember right, the train ride from post to Nuremberg is close to an hour, give or take a few. Regardless, I had never been on a train. The ride was breath taking; untouched forest, dark green pastures, small villages with mini castles made of gray stone. Germans walking amongst the villages in a slow, but content pace. After four stops in villages we made it to Nuremberg. We found our way through the train station and into old city Nuremberg.

Nuremberg is surrounded by a wall that was constructed between the twelfth century and finished in the sixteenth century. It is meant to be one of Europe's most considerable medieval defensive systems.

Inside the wall they had McDonalds, Woolworths, great big beautiful cathedrals, pubs everywhere, thousands of pigeons that were welcome anywhere, cobblestone streets, and the red light district.

Our first stop was a pub, it was August, so perfect weather to sit outside and enjoy a German beer. We were having a great time, and sure enough, what comes with thousands of pigeons that are free to roam anywhere? Exactly, a lot of pigeon poop. Unfortunately for SGT Phillipines, he was sitting close to the building underneath a drop zone. PLOP, pigeon shit landed on his head and shoulders, he sprung up like a fish out of water, and started cussing in his Philippine accent; Mudda fukka pigen, fuka bird just shiii on me, I eat dat mudda fukka pigen. We were laughing so hard my abs were hurting. Following that hilarious incident, we calmed down from laughter and moved on to another joint, not a pub, but a heavy metal bar. A long staircase led down to a dungeon like atmosphere, it was dark, smoky, and loud from the heavy metal music. Being nineteen years old, that was my kind of place. These two bars were my stomping grounds for the next three years.

In between those two bars were two of the most amazing places I have ever eaten at in my life. One was a gyro place, and even though gyro's are from Greece, this was the best I ever had. I have tried Gyro's everywhere in the States, and they just don't compare to the ones in Nuremberg. They had a lamb rotating upside down on a rotisserie, they would slice the meat off, put it in a home baked pita bread, with fresh veggies, and homemade tzatziki sauce. I will be back there one day to eat one. Directly across the cobble stone street is a place that made doner kebabs. Very similar to a gyro, but the sauces are different, it was just as delicious.

I had an amazing day and night in Nuremberg, I remember it like it was yesterday. The only bad part was, if you missed the last train to post, which we did, you had to wait until five forty four the next morning to catch the first train back to the post. I guess it wasn't that bad. Bars stayed open until four in the morning, and when they closed, a breakfast restaurant would open that served beer, or you just get beer out of a vending machine.

The train ride home from Nuremberg never changed from that first time, to the last time. The ride back to the barracks consisted of a guilty conscience of what bad stuff happened during our visit to Nuremburg, who got lost during the night, and hope they got back to the barracks, and when was the next time we were going to do it all over again. We couldn't get enough of that city.

After making it home from the train station; Sundays were usually a recovery day for most Soldier. Sleep, walks to the chow hall or Burger King, T.V, which was only one channel AFN (Armed Forces Network). I usually had a few beers while I spit shined my boots, and ironed my uniform listening to Led Zeppelin with my barracks door wide opened welcoming any passersby to come hang out. This is what most weekends consisted of in Germany, weekend trips, relax Sunday, and prepare for Monday morning formation to start the work week. I would have my gray Army physical fitness uniform laid out next to my pressed green camouflaged uniform, and my highly spit shined boots, I took a lot of pride in my Army uniforms.

Monday morning, Soldier started to gather in the parking lot, smoking cigarettes and telling stories of the weekend. Right at 0625, 1SG (First Sergeant, highest ranking Non Commissioned Officer, NCO) Yells out, FALL IN. With that command all Soldier in the company rush to their respective platoon, I was in second platoon. This time, unlike last Monday, everyone in the company was back from training, the formation was full with about seventy Soldier.

After getting accountability of all Soldier, he then asked the dreadful question, who here needs to go to sick call? There were always one or two hands that would hesitantly raise. Fall out of formation and head to sick call to get rodded dumb asses, he would say it in a father-like voice, and he made sure he embarrassed them in a civil manner.

"I am sure next time they will wear protection," 1SG said, as the two Soldier whimpered off to sick call, everyone chuckled under their breath. The rest of us began our morning workout, until 0730.

Feeling motivated and energized after a great workout we headed to our rooms to do personal hygiene and grab a quick bite to eat at the chow hall.

Mornings were pretty routine, so routine, that my room was getting worse and worse from my stinky, messy, goofy roommate. Nothing I could do about it now, but the time was coming soon for me to explode.

Besides my bad room situation, I was settled into my tank company, and comfortable with living in Germany for a few years.

DEADLY BEASTS

As 1995 came to an end we were in the field for weeks at a time training for war. The military's main focus was on Bosnia. Slobodan Milosevic was the President of Serbia/Yugoslavia at the time. From 1992 to 1995 Milosevic led a war against Bosnia to systematically remove all Bosnian Muslims. The final death toll from the years of genocide was close to one hundred thousand souls. Milosevic was put on trial for war crimes, he later died of a heart attack in his jail cell March 11th, 2006. Therefore, the war in Bosnia kept U.S Forces in Germany very busy, and always trained and ready to deploy in a moment's notice.

In order to be the best in the world, we had to train hard, and that's what we did. I finally got to do a rotation in Hohenfels Germany called CMTC (Combat Maneuver Training Center). We rail headed all of our tanks on to a train and took them to Hohenfels. We off loaded the beasts and drove through a small German town trying not to destroy buildings, Germans would weave in and out of the tanks like it was an everyday occurrence for them. On arrival we secured our tanks, found our barracks, that had no heat, no hot water, and it was the dead of winter, but I toughed it out, there wasn't no time for bitching. I was told to shower, because for the next thirty days there would be no showers. I sucked it up, held my breath, jumped in the freezing water, my junk went from small to tiny, I pounced around for about forty five seconds, got myself clean, climbed in my sleeping bag and went to sleep.

Early wakeup, we moved to our tanks to prepare to go to the 'Box'. I heard all the guys keep saying the 'Box', I finally figured out it meant the training area we were going to be in, and simulate real warfare.

A brief over view of CMTC Hohenfels; Tankers, Infantry, Aviation, a whole regiment join together to basically play laser tag with equipment called Miles Gear (Multiple Integrated laser Engagement System). We would fight battles against a Battalion of U.S Soldier called OPFOR (Opposing Force). There were also Soldier who were the equivalent to referees who made sure no side was cheating. Nonetheless, the training was as real as it gets without being in real time war.

At first I was confused as hell on what was going on, but after a week of training it clicked, I started to understand the big picture of how a battlefield is operated. It's one big machine, and if one of the links in your chain is not functioning properly i.e.... Infantry, aircraft, medics, cooks, mechanics, tankers, scouts, special forces, supply, it could all go to shit. Everyone had to work as one big team to accomplish one huge mission. With that being said, the training got pretty brutal at times.

There were nights where the temperature got down to minus thirty below, luckily, the inside of the tank was warm, and standing behind the tank was even warmer. The jet engine of the tank put out so much heat it could melt paint off a car, another advantage to the heat the tank put out, was that the back deck of the tank that covered the engine would get so hot you could warm water in your canteen cup to either eat ramen noodles or shave with. It was like your very own sixty two ton steel apartment with a built in stove and central heat. There were times the other Soldier and I had to dismount to go do roaming guard throughout the night while all tanks were parked in a huge circle.

Imagine, minus thirty below, pitch black, wearing night vision goggles, all alone patrolling the perimeter of the tanks in the middle of Germany. As you pictured that scene, did you include monsters that had curled up tusks protruding from their jaws, with jagged razor sharp teeth and a runny snot nosed pig snort making growling noises? Well besides the cold and the darkness, you had to watch for Germany's massive warthogs, they were everywhere, and they always traveled in packs. Through night vision all you could see of them were glowing eyes, followed by a black mass of enormous pig. When any of us spotted a pack of them, the best thing to do is run to the nearest tank, jump on and wait until they leave the area.

One of those times I encountered a few adults and a bunch of piglets, they must have been ten yards away from me, I panicked and ran like hell to the nearest tank. Those pigs didn't give a damn about me, but I still ran regardless. I can't remember whose tank I was on, but the pigs came to visit, and what better to do but feed them MRE's (Meals ready to eat). If MRE's are good enough for Soldier they are good enough for wild pigs. Being the Soldier that we were, we thought we might spruce it up a little and added some Caylume light (glow sticks) juice to the food, we thought maybe if they ate the MRE with glow stick juice then their poop might glow. Unfortunately, we never got to see the results.

We were constantly on the move fighting battles, repairing the tank tracks, and tons of other maintenance that was either routine or some sort of malfunction. Despite it being the number one tank in the world, it still needed a lot of work to stay in the battle.

On the other hand, part of training also meant getting killed, which sometimes we enjoyed, it gave our tank crew some down time, we could eat, clean up a little, maybe change some five day old socks and underwear and the best part about down time was getting a chance to dispose of a few days of MRE's being built up in your system. A tank wasn't equipped with a bathroom, I mean we could pee on the inside, but that's not cool for the other crew members. Each tank did come with a portable toilet, due to great Army engineering. It was a gray folded metal chair that we welded a hole in the middle of it and put tape around the rough edges so you didn't cut your butt cheeks. We would take turns, usually the highest ranking guy on the tank went first, that meant I had to pucker up for about forty five minutes before it was my turn. When we were killed by lasers our tank was dead center of the battle field, smoke used for cover and concealment filled the valley we were in, you could hear tanks and helicopters all over but couldn't see them. We were backed up to a tree line, so safe from any vehicles running us over while taking care of important business. Finally it was my turn, I had a turtle head wanting to come out bad. It was still smoky out when I leaped off the tank, I dug my small hole and cradled the chair-toilet over it. Sweating from the pressure, and scrambling to get my uniform unbuckled, I made it just in time, and wouldn't you know it, the battle we were in finished. The smoke cleared, and tanks, Bradley fighting vehicles, fuel trucks, every damn vehicle we had out there passed by on a tank trail, they all whistled, waived, and laughed as they drove by.

I joke a lot, but the training was very intense, and after thirty days or so of testing our mental and physical capacity, it was time to leave the box. The awesome thing about leaving is that our 1SG loved Popeyes Chicken, and they had a Popeyes Chicken right there on post, and holy crap, that was the best Chicken I have ever eaten in my life. Along with the amazing chicken, I was so excited to take a freezing shower as well, I had layers of stink on me.

All in all, I was feeling like a warrior, completed my very first training event and received an award for my hard work. Back at post, we had the weekend to regroup, clean our personal equipment and have some fun. So that meant a trip to Nuremberg, beer, gyros, and German girls.

I began to hang out with three guys from my company, we became real good friends; the first guy (F1) was a by the book guy when he wasn't drinking, but soon as he had that one beer, shit hit the fan. The second guy (F2) had a passion for boxing and fighting, so you can imagine how that went after a few beers, but he was also a lover. They both were skinny, had brown hair, and probably could have passed as brothers. Then there was the last guy (F3), he was the oldest of the group, sophisticated, Florida State graduate, and was always keeping the three of us out of trouble, or sometimes he was the silent instigator for us to do stupid shit.

We had another successful trip to Nuremberg that weekend. I don't want to get into details, Nuremberg trips alone would be a whole other book, but just know, it was always a blast. Matter of fact the trip was so successful that F2 met his future wife, and my lifelong friend (LLF) at the Green Goose, a beautiful German girl, down to earth and an amazing woman. As for the rest of us meeting girls, well let's just leave that to the readers imagination.

Back to the barracks, we had the same Sunday mission…to prepare for Monday and the week ahead. This week we were headed to Grafenwöhr (Graf). It's a training area that backs up to the post, so basically we roll our tanks out the back fence of our motor pool (Motor Pool, where we keep and maintain our vehicles) and we are in the training area. The difference between Hohenfels and Graf, Graf is a live fire training area, so we shoot live rounds, Hohenfels is a battle maneuver training area, without live rounds, just laser tag. Nonetheless, I was pumped to go blow shit up.

Cold winter morning, we rolled the beasts out to the firing range, our minds were continuously rehearsing our specific job we had to accomplish without error inside the tank. I went from being a loader to driving the tank. There are four crewman per tank, loader, driver, gunner and then the tank commander (TC), every position is just as important as the other.

On standby waiting on instructions from the tower, we were talking and joking inside the tank. The driver seat is separate from the rest of the crew. The jobs of the loader, PVT M, gunner, SGT P, and TC, SSG B, were to focus on the enemy and kill them, my job was to listen to every command of the TC and execute flawlessly. This is how it could sound inside a tank:

"Reed you doing okay in the drivers hole?" the TC asks.

"Yeah Sarge," I reply.

"You must be good Reed, because I could smell your cigarette smoke up here in the Turret"

"Oh Shit," I thought to myself as I cracked the drivers hatch and nervously flicked it out.

Then I hear laughter over our CVC helmets (Combat Vehicle Crewman), TC comes back on.

"Ohhh Reed, I don't give a shit Lil Dawwgg, we are up here smoking as well"

Then the tower radio's in, A22, scan your lane blah blah blah, I can't remember the exact words from the tower, but it was time to execute, all joking and smoking put to rest, it was game time.

TC gets confirmation from the crew, "Driver you up?"

"Roger Sarge," I reply, as nervous adrenaline sweat starts to pour out my forehead.

"Loader you up?" No answer. "LOADER WAKE THE FUCK UP," as a left back hand comes flying across the tank and smacks PVT M in the arm.

"YEAH SARGE, SHIT, YEAH I AM UP."

"Okay good, stay with us, gunner you up?"

"Yes, I am good to go." The gunner mumbles as he looks through his scope making last minute adjustments on the 120MM Main Gun.

"Driver move out." That was my command to start to drive down the range road keeping a pace of about twenty miles per hour while the rest of the crew scanned the battlefield for pop-up tank targets or pop-up troop targets.

"GUNNER, SABOT, TANK," the TC yelled.

"INDENTIFIED," the gunner replied.

"UP," the loader shouted as he slammed a forty nine pound armor piercing round into the main gun.

"FIRE," the TC ordered.

"ON THE WAY," as the gunner pulled the trigger. BOOOOOOMMMMMM, the blast from the tank blinded me with smoke and dust, but I just had to stay calm, drive straight and hold my speed steady until my vision was clear again. As the tank fires the blast is so powerful it lifts your uniform off your body and the hatches on the tank slightly jump open, windows within a few miles shake, if too close it will blow out windows on a car.

"Target," the TC announced. "Great job fellas," and we continued on down range shooting targets. What a great feeling.

That was it for that day, it's a day you wish you could sit back and say let's have a beer and reminisce on the days training. Unfortunately we couldn't do that, we had to be ready for the next day, which consisted of each platoon rolling down a range shooting together, and it is a day that is tattooed in my brain forever.

Early morning, fourteen tanks lined one side of a gravel road, another fourteen lined the other side. It was quiet and calm but cold, all the tanks were shutdown except auxiliary power which kept radio's on and still gave power to the tanks. We all dismounted the beasts and started making our way to the tower for the days safety briefing. As we passed one of the tanks I noticed a guy in the TC hatch rotating the turret and the main gun, and below the main gun the drivers hatch was opened. I didn't think anything of it, he was just doing some last minute checks probably.

There was a group of Soldier about ten feet behind my group, and all of the sudden we hear a disturbed loud voice yell, HOLY FUCK STOP STOP STOP, NOOOOO, STOP, it was too late. That tank with the guy up in the TC hatch had crushed his drivers head with part of the turret and the main gun, they had their helmets on but were not communicating between each other. It was the most gruesome thing I had ever witnessed, and out of respect for the family I am not going to get into details.

There was no mourning, no taking time to recover over what just happened. A medevac helicopter, and a small track ambulance, came and recovered his body. A quick investigation took place, the officer in charge of the range had the lowest ranking guys clean the remains of the Soldier off the front slope of the tank.

After the air and ground ambulances departed, we continued our day, obviously we had a longer than usual safety briefing. My crew mounted our tank, and we sat in silence for over an hour waiting on our turn to fire.

Finally, my TC's voice comes across the CVC helmets, "you guys okay?"

I replied with a low voice, "Yeah Sarge, I am good."

M says, "I don't know, that was fucked up man." He was still in shock, but I think we all were, people just handle situations like that differently.

Our company had finished the day firing and headed back to post, the rest of the week was very somber. We continued to work, still recovering from Hohenfels, and Graf, we held the Soldier funeral, and laid him to rest.

Pushing forward, and trying not to forget, but to come to terms with the accident, a huge change of events was heading our direction, and we were motivated and ready for our adventure. It was early 1996, our 1SG and Commander held a formation and broke the news to us.

We were to start training on infantry tactics, because we were deploying to Macedonia in April, leaving our tanks in Germany, and becoming the first tank Battalion to perform an Infantry mission. Of course us tankers thought to ourselves, damnit we have to walk places.

Along with doing our infantry training, I was selected to travel to Germany for a couple of weeks and help train Soldier going to Bosnia, it was a good mission. I got to wear civilian clothes, act as a civilian on the battlefield, and harass Soldier at training compounds.

Not only were we training hard, but a lot of changes took place for our company and the Army itself. One of the changes, or additions, were two Drill Sergeants from Ft Knox, who had just finished their tours as Drill Sergeants, came to our Company. SFC (Sergeant First Class) Hero 1 (H1) was put in charge of second platoon, my platoon, and SFC Hero 2 (H2) was put in charge of third platoon.

At first everyone was like oh shit, these two are going to be the biggest assholes on the face of the Earth, I mean why wouldn't they be? They are ex-Drill Sergeants. It turns out they were two of the humblest, laid back platoon SGT's a Soldier could ask for. They were well respected, and took their positions serious, and treated us with respect, unless you were a Lieutenant (Civilian definition of Lieutenant-annoying manager who thinks they know everything and tries to re-invent the wheel), no one likes Lieutenants...except Lieutenants.

The other change was that of our divison, we were changing over from 3rd Infantry Division, to 1st Infantry Division, The Big Red One. Instead of our Company being 2/37 Armor we were becoming 2/67 Armor. I remember that day well. Hundreds of Soldier stood in formation for hours in the freezing cold, but were disciplined and proud of the change.

The day came, after months of preparation we were trained and motivated for our mission to Macedonia.

MACEDONIA

Elbow to elbow, we were packed in a C-130 Air Force cargo plane. Heads hung down, not as a sign of depression, but to rest the mind, the sounds of the roaring engines were calming. Riding in a military vehicle, or aircraft before a mission is therapeutic, it's a time to prepare yourself mentally for what is to come.

As I sat there staring into the pallet of equipment that lined the middle of the plane, I struggled to retrieve my Walkman from the cargo pocket of my uniform. I donned the foam headphones and adjusted the thin metal head band over my crew cut hair, and smashed down the play button, it played, "Run to the hills, run for your li-iiiifffee," it was Iron Maiden. I laid my head back, gently closed my eyes, and with my breath at a slow pace I drifted off to sleep.

We touched down in Macedonia a few hours later, it was basically a straight flight south from Germany. A few buses took us to our post called Uniform 9, it was ran by the United Nations, so all vehicles were painted white, and our head gear was a baby blue color.

The buildings were from WWll, they had holes of different sizes from remnants of tank rounds and other weapons. Our barracks had been condemned for decades, rodents, spiders and cute little hedgehogs had taken up occupancy in the buildings. Rust settled in on the showers, sinks and toilets. The only air conditioning was from the dirt covered window screens when they were propped open and let a nice breeze in. Besides all that it wasn't really that bad, we had old bunks, with dust covered mattresses, running water, and lots of brooms to start clean up and make it home.

Throughout the rest of the post we had a small trailer that only civilians worked at, it was our shoppette. It had, the essentials, toiletries, beer, tobacco, snacks, and back then there was no internet, so yes, playboy magazines were sold. Across the street from the shoppette was a small bar and pizza place called the Gator Inn, it got a little wild at times. Down the street we had a couple huge aircraft hangars that were used for a gym, basketball courts, and a boxing ring, the other hangar was our chow hall. Lastly, we had a nice big field for football and other games.

Uniform 9 was the main post; our other homes were several observation posts that lined the Serbian border. We rotated every few weeks, from Uniform 9 to our post along the Serbian border.

After getting settled in to our condemned barracks 1SG asked for volunteers to head out to an Observation Post (OP) with another company a few weeks before our company were to take over. I quickly raised my hand, and was on my way the following day.

My Post was Uniform 54 (U54); constantine wire and sand bags lined the area, bunkers were set up on each side of the compound, a tower stood tall on one end of the compound that overlooked the Serbian border, we manned it twenty four hours a day. It had five connexes, four for housing three Soldier a piece, and one for dry non-perishable food. There was a small workout room attached to our kitchen and an eating area that was equipped with a tube TV in which we were able to get our one channel, AFN. To run all this, we had generators for electricity, water that was brought to us which we had to ration, food that was flown in or trucked in every week or so. We had to cook our own meals, and worked together to keep the compound in a maintained clean area. Everyone had their duty, if it were filling the generators, cleaning the showers, cooking, guard duty or radio watch, we all made it happen.

After three weeks of being on the OP, my platoon finally made it and relieved the other company I was with. There were eleven of us all together that lived on the OP for weeks at a time. Here are their names starting with the highest ranking to the lowest; the Platoon SGT, SFC H1, he was the boss, pretty much our dad, then SSG PR, he was mild, toned laid back guy from Puerto Rico, next was SGT F3 from Florida, and SGT

Philippines (Pigeon poo SGT), and then the metro-sexual of the platoon SGT MS, he was a ladies man, always tan. SPC Stinky was our medic, he was suppose to make sure everyone kept up with hygiene, but ironically he had the worst smelling feet, and he would walk around the OP acting out scenes from the movie *Full Metal Jacket*, then there was SPC Nerd, the black kid with glasses who liked to sleep a lot, his bunk mate and OP wife was PVT FOS, strictly because they argued a lot, he was a tall in shape kid that was messy as hell and smelly, maybe him and Stinky were having a competition! SFC H1 had to force him to shower, he also thought he was Gods gift to women. Then, there was my good friend SPC Mafia, he was the heavy metal, deep east coast accent wanna be from New York, and our guard dog Bear, he was mean as hell, he only liked people in uniform. Nonetheless, despite our different personalities and backgrounds, these guys were my family. Being isolated on the OP for weeks at a time, with no phones, stores, or any kind of civilization we had to stay positive and rely on one another to stay sane. Along with relying on each other there were also two events that took place that summer back in the states that helps bring meaning to why Soldier fight for our freedom everyday all over the globe.

The first event was the Colorado Avalanche winning the Stanley Cup, I remember being on guard duty in the tower when SFC H1 yelled up at me saying the Avalanche just won the cup, it was an awesome feeling having your hometown team win a championship.

Following the Stanley Cup, were the summer Olympics of 1996 in Atlanta. Despite the heartless act of Eric Rudolph setting off a bomb that year, the Olympics continued, and it was incredible to watch the young, talented women's gymnastics team, 'The Magnificent Seven'. The young ladies were the first women's gymnastics team to ever bring home the Gold. It was so powerful and heart warming being in a foreign land protecting freedom, and watching these young girls perform for our great country, it truly brought tears to my eyes to watch them compete and win. They inspired me to do my best while serving in the Army.

When we weren't watching sports or lounging around, we had to send a team of four Soldier once a day to conduct patrols through local villages either on foot or mounted in vehicles. Our mission was basically to monitor and record any unusual activities with the local population. During patrols it got a little heated with children swarming us as we patrolled through villages, trying to grab our M16's or other equipment, we had to be alert at all times. Always have your head on a swivel they would say. They also would ask us for pens and candy, so when we left on patrol, we would make sure we stocked up on pens and candy to hand out.

The Macedonia people were very poor, it was a third world country. They live in huts, they farm, all laundry and washing are done in the local river, very few had electricity. There was one patrol where we had to go downtown Skopje. I picture this in my head to this day, as we passed a young woman holding a baby, flies swarmed the babies head and she was begging for help, I glanced at her and the lifeless bundle, and realized the he was dead. As emotional as it was to see her stand there holding her baby, tears flowing down her face begging for help, there was nothing I could do, we just had to keep patrolling. I prayed for her throughout my life.

Following a day of patrols and area beautification we had some downtime on the OP, we played a lot of poker, I used to piss SFC H1 off all the time because I would take his money. While playing poker we would also cook our own meals, we brought lots of seasonings. Our main protein source was a slabs of kangaroo meat that was so tough it was like trying to eat a rubber tire, but we used our imaginations at always put together good meals with what we had to work with. All of our left overs went to a local farmer. He would come every few days and would stand outside the perimeter holding a clear liquid bottle waiting for us to notice him. We gave him our slop bucket so he could feed his pigs, in return the clear liquid bottle was pure Macedonian Moon Shine. I will leave it to the readers imagination of what happened when drinking moon shine, put it this way, SPC Mafia was blind for a day.

Part of being on a Peace Keeping mission includes lots of visits from dignitaries. The Secretary of Defense William Perry visited us, a lot of Senators and Generals, my favorite of them all was General A. We knew he was coming to visit, we cleaned the compound, made it spotless, replaced ripped sand bags, made sure our boots were shined, and uniforms were clean, and we also made sure SPC Gossett washed his stinky ass feet and forced PVT FOS to shower. They wanted us to prepare a good meal as well, if I remember right, we made spaghetti. The day came, we were looking sharp and professional. The black hawk (UH 60 Helicopter) landed on a small helipad just up from our front gate, SFC H1 and Bear met the General and his entourage at the gate. Our Brigade Commander was a Full Bird Colonel, he was a tall stout black man with a small afro that was nearly out of regulation, and he had it juiced nice. He was intimidating, never smiled, and had a fierce look about him.

SFC H1 escorted the group around the OP, and then made it to our dining area to eat. All of us Soldier were standing silently around the table, as they walked in SFC H1 yelled attention, we all snap to the command, head and eyes straight forward, arms down to the side, with fingers slightly rolled, heels touching and boots pointed out in a forty five degree angle.

"Relax gentleman," General A commanded, he started going around the table getting to know the Soldier, and then it was my turn. "Hey there PVT Reed, you look like Barney Rubble," he said, as we shook hands.

I replied, "Hey there General A, you look like Fred Flintstone".

It was silent, I saw SFC H1, silently lean his head back, eyes rolled, and with no voice just a mouth movement he said fuuuccckkk.

The Colonel's eyes got as big as golf balls, his neck stiffened up so fast and hard, I thought his jerry curl was going spring from his tiny afro and splatter the walls. After a moment of silence from the shock of me calling a three-star General Fred Flintstone, General A began to laugh.

He said "I like you Reed," that moment relaxed everyone while we sat and ate.

Most high-ranking individuals and great leaders don't like ass kissers, some do. I was never much of an ass kisser, maybe a great manipulator, but not an ass kisser, so I think General A respected that. He didn't mind me calling him Flintstone.

Our time came to rotate back to U9 for a couple of weeks, I remember Friday nights were boxing nights, Soldier were allowed to get in a ring together with gloves and beat the crap out of each other while we downed several beers.

We would also gather at the Gator bar to drink and socialize. Woody Harrelson and Marisa Tomei were actually there one evening to have drinks, they were filming the movie *Welcome to Sarajevo*. I wasn't around to see them, I had actually just left with three of my friends to take our two weeks of leave in Greece, and it was a blast.

We hopped on a train down to Greece from Macedonia, we had a stop in the middle of the night at a train station in southern Macedonia. The four of us were starving. Luckily, I was a professional at negotiating on foreign lands, well at least that's what my drunk inner self used to tell me. We sat at a table, the waiter brought us our menus, and it was not in English, so of course I told the fellas, ya'll just wait here, I got this one. I approached the bar area and held up four fingers and pointed at a beer. Then I rubbed my belly and held up four fingers, and he pointed to a cat that was sprawled across the floor. I shook my head yes and smiled. He smiled as well and held up four fingers, I thought damn that's cheap, four beers, four cats for four dollars, that's better than McDonalds.

I sat back down and the guys asked me how it went?

I said "great, we will have four steaks, and four beers here in a few minutes." Now I don't know if it was really cat or not, but needless to say it was an amazing little steak, the guys loved it as well. I paid the four dollars and we headed back to the train. They asked me what kind of meat it was, I told them cat, they laughed and thought I was joking.

Our next and last stop was the border of Macedonia and Greece, it was mid-morning and hot as balls, we got out and went through customs. Back then Soldier didn't need passports, we just needed our military identification cards to travel around the world.

We made it to a city called Thessaloniki, from there we sardined ourselves on a hot non-air-conditioned bus and drove down to our final destination, a beach resort town called Kallithea, and dang, I was in Heaven.

I have been to the ocean once before, but nothing like the ocean off Greece. The water was so blue, the sky mirrored it with speckles of white clouds that seemed to glow, they were so white. Soft sand lined the ocean shore for miles, everyone walked around in bathing suits and flip flops. Bars were placed in the middle of century old gladiator stadiums. Endless fresh fruit, beer and fried cheese with lemon splashed on it was my diet for the next two weeks. I also found the meaning to Greek Goddesses, the Greek women were some of the most beautiful women I have ever seen, golden brown skin with dark hair. I was definitely in paradise.

We managed to find two rooms right on the beach for ten dollars a night. The dollar was worth significantly more than the Greek Drachma, that was back then, now it is entirely different with Europe transitioning to the Euro.

For those two weeks it was party until the sun came up, sleep for a few hours, head to the beach, eat fruit and cheese, and then repeat. The final day we were there, F1 and I were at an outside restaurant, we couldn't stomach anymore beer or alcohol, so we slammed water, and ate fruit. F1 tried pouring water out of a pitcher into a glass but was shaking so hard from withdrawals he spilled it everywhere. We were definitely strung out from vacation, and the worse part was that we had to go back to reality.

Back at U9, our friend F2 returned from leave, he ended up marrying LLF from Nuremberg on his two-weeks leave, we were all very happy for them. Now that everyone was back, we did a couple more rotations to the OP before heading back to Germany. The night before we flew back, we had a drink fest at the Gator bar, it was one hell of a party, and the next day suuucccckkkeeeddd. It was by far the worst flight I have ever taken, I was so hungover I honestly didn't think I would make it. I told myself, just like many millions of people have told themselves after a night of hardcore drinking, I am never drinking again, yeah…that lasted a day.

So back to the barracks after a long day of traveling, I opened my room to stale cigarette smoke and a mildew smell. No one had been in there for over six months. I was getting stuff put away when I heard F1 yell my name from down the hallway.

"Reed, get yo' ass down here!" I walked down to his and F2's room and he said "you remember this?" It was a full Budweiser beer can we all signed and left on their desk, and before we left for Macedonia we agreed to all slam it when we got home. So, that's what we did, a warm, probably year-old beer, we drank and passed it around until it was all gone. Not sure what happened to that beer can.

Recovery from our trip to Macedonia took up the next few weeks and then it was back to the same routine of tanking, drinking, playing basketball, spades and dominos.

The bad part of returning to Germany is that I still had Messy Smurf as a roommate, and I couldn't take it anymore. He would stand in his boxers picking at his ass, and the room was always a mess, so I begged 1SG Legend and SFC H1 to let me move rooms. I already had it planned out, I was to stay with SPC R2, he was a laid-back clean guy. 1SG and SFC H1 agreed to let me move, I was excited. SPC R2s mom would send him VHS tapes of South Park, it was just coming out. All of us throughout the barracks would gather around and watch episode after episode. I was definitely happy with my new roommate, we got along great.

At this point of my tour in Germany I was a little over half way done, and I realized I haven't traveled that much, or seen parts of Germany except Nuremburg. Therefore, I made it a point to make it to October Fest in Munich, and holy shit was it fun. The Hofbräuhaus tent was packed with Germans on the table cheering and singing 'Ein pro-zit, Der Germutlichkeit, meaning 'Salute to our cozy friendship and good times we are having together'. Banners hung down from the ceiling tent of legendary music artists from the sixties through the nineties that had ever played there. Everyone one from Janis Joplin, to The Beatles, you name it they played there.

Another place I was able to visit was Euro Disneyland in France, some of us took a trip there for New Year's 1996 into 1997. Although its not as big and glamorous as Disneyworld it was still worth the trip. A few months later about ten of us took another trip to Paris. I went up the Eifel Tower, visited the Louvre Museum, and after forcing my way through hundreds of tourists taking pictures, I was able to snap one picture of the Mona Lisa, but it didn't came out when I had the film developed. I heard it has a two-inch-thick bullet proof glass, and a certain lighting that deters cameras from taking pictures. Nonetheless, it was amazing to see. To top off the trip to Paris I was absolutely amazed with the King and Queens palace. The royal jewelry, and paintings throughout the palace were breath taking, its amazing what was done so long ago without technology, I like all natural so much more.

Paris is beautiful, but I had one other country I visited that I hope I never go back to. The country was Czechoslovakia (Czech); F1, F2, F3, myself and I am sure a few other Soldier did a weekend in Nuremburg. After drinking all night and having a great time, we caught the early morning train back to post. When the train arrived on post, apparently F1 and F2 said they tried to wake me up but I was more or less unconscious. They said I took a swing at them, but I was so drunk I don't remember any of this, so being the great friends, they were, they said fuck you Reed, and left me on the train. The next thing I remember is waking up with so much pain in my shoulder, and it was because the Czech police were pulling me off the train in a hog tie. I had ended up in Czech, they searched me and found out I was a Soldier. They called my 1SG, and put me back on the train to Germany, and 1SG Legend picked me up from the train station. I was embarrassed, but 1SG Legend was such a great guy and leader, he didn't punish me, he just took me back to the barracks and said he would see me Monday.

In between traveling we still had to train, I finally had my own tank. Usually it's the driver's tank, he is the one that maintains it the most and makes sure it is always ready to go. We got to name our tanks as well, the name had to start with an 'A' since we were Alpha Company. Being from the county named Arapahoe, I proudly named my tank Arapahoe.

For the last time, I sat in Arapahoe, anxiously waiting our turn to go shoot, we qualified our tank with a little over nine hundred points. This is significant because tradition is, if you don't qualify on a tank with a nine hundred or above you don't get wear the tanker boots. The tanker boot stands out from any other boot in the Army/military. If a Soldier is wearing them you know he is a tanker. Any Soldier can wear jump boots, or infantry boots, but only a tanker can wear tanker boots. My pair of tank boots were given to me by 1SG Legend, I still have those boots, and I have kept them shined for twenty three years. RIP 1SG Legend, you were an incredible father, leader, 1SG, husband, and a Soldier friend, you are missed.

I was getting close to my tour being up, I had to make a choice, either reenlist and stay in Germany, or get out and go back to the states. As much as I loved Germany, and all the great friendships, and brotherhood that had formed, I missed the U.S. I missed the simple things; driving, grocery stores, Taco Bell, more than one channel, I missed watching sports, and most of all I missed Colorado.

My last few weeks in Germany, the Denver Broncos won the Super Bowl against the Green Bay Packers. Yes, I am a Dolphins fan, but I still support my home town team, so it was cool to see them win. I believe the game started just after one in the morning in Germany, so we were up all night gathered around SGT F3's tube TV watching the game. Fortunately, they gave us Monday off, so that was nice.

Then on February 14th, Valentine's day 1998, I flew back to the United States. It was bitter sweet, I was sad to leave, but happy to go home. I miss all my brothers from A Co 2/63 Armor Avengers, you will always be with me. All different backgrounds, all different color, all different personalities, but all with the same purpose. Love you guys.

I HAD IT ALL

Once back home, I quickly got myself an apartment, a vehicle and some nice new furniture. I was living large, I managed to save up a lot of money in Germany, and during my deployment to Macedonia. I didn't have anything to spend it on Macedonia except for poker games. I was debt free, single, and not a care in the world. I was still getting paid from the Army for a couple of months using up all my leave time, so I didn't work right away, I partied like a rock star. Sadly, it came time to become an adult and start work before my funds ran out.

I landed a job back at the Grease Monkey, there wasn't much else I was qualified for, but it was a respectful job, and I worked with some great guys. I also decided I needed some education, so I used my GI Bill and started going to community college for law enforcement. In addition, I was assigned to a Signal Unit for the National Guard, which was just like the commercials says, 'one weekend a month, two weeks a year'. That was true before 9-11 happened. To top it off I started delivering pizzas for Dominos. I stayed busy day and night, and still found time to drink and party.

The unfortunate thing about working two jobs, going to school and drinking like I did, is that I wore myself out. I slowly transitioned from a hardworking adult, to a functioning alcoholic.

My drinking and partying caught up with me, before long I was broke, living pay check to pay check. I lived off of Hunt's spaghetti sauce, Top Ramen noodles, peanut butter, bread and milk. I ask myself all the time, why do you find the need to drink constantly, I hated myself for it. There were many times I contemplated committing suicide. I was in a dark part of my life. I hated who I had become.

At work, I would vacuum cars and steal change from the car just so I could get something for lunch, I drank during class, and while delivering pizzas. I was always hungover, I was a mess.

As I was spiraling down, I remember sitting in my apartment April 20th, 1999 and breaking news came across the television, the biggest, deadliest school shooting took place at Columbine High School, just miles away from me. After seeing the footage of that horrific day, I couldn't possibly feel sorry for myself or where I had put myself in life. I absolutely cannot imagine what the parents and the students went through and what they are still going through to this day. Unfortunately, I believe Columbine was the beginning to an era of mass shootings. As the healing process took place in Colorado, and the shock wore off from the shooting, I continued to destroy myself.

Then July 7th, 2000, exactly ten years to the day, I was with Maxwell. We were leaving a local bar, and I ended up going through a checkpoint and got slapped with a DWAI (Driving While Abilities Impaired). It was 9 PM. The guy that put me in handcuffs was in one of my law enforcement classes, he was training that night. I was pissed. But it was no one's fault but my own. Maxwell, walked away scotch free once again, this would be the second time I got arrested with him. Needless to say, I will never hang out with him again on July 7th.

There I was, I had hit rock bottom. How was I going to pull myself out of this one? DWAI's are expensive. I had to do alcohol classes, community service, my license was suspended, insurance went up. My only option was to man up and deal with the consequences. So, I did, I kept pushing forward.

The next year of my life went by and I was able to put that DWAI behind me. Don't drink and drive, it messes up your life, and you can easily hurt yourself or someone else. Now-a-days there is no excuse, all you have to do is call Lyft or Uber.

Despite my drinking and bad decisions, I had made after being home from Germany, life was about to start looking up for me. I got a full time technician job with the National Guard. Which entails we were the uniform every day, but we were not 'considered' active duty. It was a great start to a federal job in hopes of having a decent retirement someday. My job was driving a semi, I would take Army equipment all over the state, and sometimes to Wyoming, I actually enjoyed it quite a bit. I still managed to take college courses in my spare time, I switched from law enforcement to fire science. I obviously didn't care to much for law enforcement after my DWAI.

I started pulling myself out of debt, and was somewhat stable, I was getting paid eleven dollars an hour, which to me was a lot compared to the nine dollars an hour at Grease Monkey. Life was getting good, so good I met my first wife (X-Wife).

MAS

It was a Tuesday, normal day at work, and the country was just attacked by terrorists, the deadliest attack on American soil since Pearl Harbor. At first, we thought it was an accident, but as the day went on, we all learned it was an act of war against the U.S. All government buildings were closed after the attacks, we were sent home. Our government and military rapidly reacted to Afghanistan and annihilated most of the Taliban, but this was a different war, the war against terrorism sadly will never end. There has always been, and always will be evil people in the world.

After 9-11 took place it changed the way of a National Guard Soldier. We as guard members became more applicable to deployments, not only were we serving the state, we had to step up and serve in war as well. It was just a matter of time before my unit was called up to deploy, but until that happened, I continued my life.

X-Wife and I moved in together, and before we knew it, we were getting married. The wedding was a blast. F2 and LLF, from Germany, as well as F1 and his wife attended the wedding, it was quite the party. We took our honeymoon in Cancun, that was an awesome time as well, snorkeling, jungle tour, and endless tequila. The day we left Cancun, we were at the airport, broke as hell, we literally had enough money for one Gatorade to share, so I guess you could say we managed our money just right.

What follows a honeymoon? A baby, we were pregnant, and very happy about it. I was mentally prepared, and ready for the journey of being a dad, X-Wife called me at work one day, and told me she had been bleeding a lot. We lost our first baby. I wasn't prepared for a miscarriage, I never even thought something like that could happen to us, but it did, and I cannot imagine the emotions, a woman goes through during a miscarriage. We got through it by telling ourselves that it wasn't meant to be, there was something seriously wrong with the baby. Not that we ever recovered from the miscarriage, because I will always remember that day, but we were able to get pregnant again, and this time it was right, and in July 2004, my son (MAS) was born. My best friend, my hero, I look up to him more than anyone in the world.

The night he was born was magical and scary at the same time. X-Wife ended up having a C-section. They drugged her good, she was out of it, I was in the operating room as well. As they did the procedure, I remember blood being slung everywhere, it was like watching a Saw movie. But I was able to stomach it, they pulled my son out and I heard his cry, I was teary eyed. The nurse asked if I wanted to cut the umbilical cord, and I said hell yeah. It was like cutting through a raw bratwurst, I had to take several attempts at it, but I got'er done. Next, the nurse asked me to carry him down to the nursery. It was the middle of the night I had been up forever, and she wanted me to walk this baby down a long hallway.

I said to her, "well that's not a good idea, I am tired as hell,"

She said, "don't be a bitch, take your son and carry him to the nursery". She handed him to me and I walked him to the nursery, all that was going through my head was, don't drop him, don't drop him, don't drop him, I made it safely. The nurse said, good job daddy, I felt great after that, I was officially a dad.

Our next move after MAS was born was purchasing a home. X-Wife worked for the mortgage business and told me it was not a good time to buy. I should have listened to her, lenders were giving loans out to anyone and everyone at the time, and it back fired a few years later. Still we ended up purchasing a home, I was excited to own my first home.

Unfortunately, I wasn't able to help move any of my furniture into the new home, I had to have my buddies do all the work.

A few weeks before that I was playing in a recreation league basketball game, and took off down the court on a fast break and a defender jumped in from of me. My leg planted but my body kept going, and all I heard was POP POP POP, I laid there in agonizing pain. As I looked up, I could see the crowd in shock, the whole bottom part of my leg went sideways. The end results were a torn ACL, MCL, and partially torn meniscus. For about six months I was pretty much useless. The mental impact an injury like that takes on your mind is the hardest part to overcome, the physical part will eventually come naturally.

2005 rolled around, the war in Afghanistan, and Iraq continued. Here on the homeland the costliest hurricane ever recorded hit our southern coast. It caused major destruction all the way from Florida to Texas, Louisiana suffered the most devastation.

As a National Guard member, we were called up to help support the rescue missions in Louisiana. I was now part of an Aviation unit, that had Chinook, Blackhawk and Huey helicopters, I ran the fuel program for the Aviation Unit. We deployed several helicopters down to that region, I stayed in my home state and helped set up tents and supply water for displaced refugees that were brought to our state. The entire country was affected by this mean hurricane.

A lot was happening, war, hurricanes, recovering from surgery, I was enjoying MAS, watching him grow up so fast, and my marriage took a turn downhill. As fast as we got married was as fast as we separated. I don't know what it was, maybe I wasn't ready for marriage, maybe it was my drinking, but I just didn't want to be married, I wasn't happy. I just didn't feel a connection between us, I honestly think we might have jumped into a marriage way to fast.

With MAS about a year old we separated, I felt horrible, and felt like a failure, but everything happens for a reason.

X-Wife moved her and MAS into an apartment, I kept the house, she didn't want anything to do with it, and she was smart about that. They only lived a few miles away, I saw him every morning, I took him to day care on the Air Force Base where I worked. X-Wife and I have kept it cordial of the years, no animosity between us, and MAS has taken it well.

Now it was my time, with the war going on in the middle east, my Aviation Battalion was called on to go to Iraq, for a total of eighteen months, six months in FT Hood, Texas for training, and twelve months in Iraq.

Before I left, I rented out my house, and made sure all paperwork for MAS and X-Wife was taken care of, we were still married but separated for the time being, so if anything were to happen to me, they would be set.

The day came to get on a bus to FT Hood, Texas, X-Wife and MAS dropped me off, MAS was almost two at the time, and I could tell he knew what was going on. I grabbed him out of his car seat, and hugged him, he started crying and put his arms around my neck. It was the hardest day of my life to leave him, but it's a part of being in the military.

IRAQ

FT Hood, Texas, 'The Great Place' they called it, we unloaded the buses, and all the pilots and air crew were housed right away. The fuelers, cooks and mechanics, we were always last to be taken care of, we sat on our duffle bags for six hours in the Texas heat waiting on barracks to move in to. They finally found us some rooms, they were condemned barracks, disgusting, they smelled, rust and graffiti covered the rooms, the toilets were stained, but we dealt with it, the good part was that we were away from all the high-ranking people, so we had some wild nights. We named our barracks the ghetto.

We were the biggest National Guard Unit to deploy to Iraq, we had attachments from Nebraska, Minnesota, and a few from other states. The Chinook guys flew missions with Special Ops, the Blackhawk guys moved dignitaries, and the other Blackhawk company were our medevac guys, we also had a company of Apache attack helicopters attached to us. To support all that we had my platoon who fueled aircraft, the cooks and ground mechanics who worked on vehicles, and a helicopter maintenance company that worked on the helicopters, and of course admin people who took care of, or screwed up our paperwork. It was a pretty big operation, and I was proud to be part of it.

This time was different from when I was in Germany and Macedonia, because of technology. I purchased my first cell phone ever, it was a flip phone, I was high roller. I put in a lot of people's numbers and I learned what a text was, it took me a while to figure it out, but I did. One of the texts I received said LOL, it was from a female, for about a year I thought LOL meant lots of love, so I thought she liked me. I was wrong about that, laughing out loud. Nonetheless, I was able to keep in better contact with MAS, so that made me feel not so far from home. When I was in Macedonia, we waited weeks just to get a letter, now we could just text and email.

Training was completed at FT Hood, we were trained up and ready to go do our year long mission in Iraq, I was happy to get out of FT Hood, it was so damn hot, I always thought it was hotter than Iraq. We were able to go home for a week before heading to Iraq, I stayed at hotel in Denver and spent quality time with MAS, and then I had to say good bye again. It never gets easy saying good bye to love ones when you are leaving for long periods of time.

We boarded a commercial airline and started the journey to Kuwait; all of our equipment was shipped over by boat. The last leg of the flight we flew over Baghdad, I looked out the window and on each side of our plane there were Air Force fighter jets escorting our plane across Iraq, it was awesome, and when you look down on Baghdad you could see bright flashes and fires everywhere. It was definitely a war zone.

We landed in Kuwait in the middle of the night, it was so hot, and it had a Southern Texas oil smell to it. We loaded the buses and headed to Camp Buehring Kuwait for two weeks to get acclimated to the time change before we headed up north to Iraq. After two weeks of ridiculous politics at Camp Buehring we packed into a C-130 and made our hot, uncomfortable plane ride into Camp Anaconda, Balad Iraq. As the plane reached the inside of the perimeter of Camp Anaconda, we were approximately thirty thousand feet in the air circling the Post, I put on my Ipod touch and started playing Led Zeppelin "Stairway to Heaven". The plane dropped fast, it swirled in a downward spiral, staying within the perimeter of Camp Anaconda. It was like the greatest roller coaster ride ever, my stomach was in my throat, my heart was pounding, flares were shot out from the plane to deter any enemy fire, and nine minutes into the song, we landed smoothly on the ground.

Camp Anaconda was nothing like I expected, it was huge, had swimming pools, a movie theatre, nice gyms and basketball courts, a great chow hall, and a nice big PX (PX=Equivalent to a Walgreen's). Despite the nice amenities, we were mortared on a daily basis. The post had a nickname, 'Mortarittaville'. The Iraqis would freeze the rockets at night, and when it warmed up during the day they would start to launch into the compound, they weren't very accurate at all, and most of them got shot down by huge Gatling guns that looked like a water hose when in sprayed bullets to shoot down the rockets before they impacted anywhere. A few times they were lucky and were able to penetrate the compound. As I was walking to the gym, and I hear a distinct loud whistle getting louder and louder as it got closer, I looked up and saw for rockets whizzing by me and a few seconds later they detonated by our ground maintenance area. There were only minor shrapnel injuries, but it could have been a lot worse.

For that year, besides dodging mortars, I was in charge of a rotation out to a FARP (Forward Area Refueling Point). This consisted of an area with fuel hoses laid out from a fuel truck that reached out across several helipads, It's purpose was for rapid refueling so helicopters do not have to shut down, they just refuel and hurry up to continue their mission. Nights were the busiest times, that is when most missions took place. There was one night in an eight-hour period we filled seventy nine aircraft, that was a record. The U.S and allies were doing a huge push into Baghdad, so to stay in the fight they needed fuel, and that was our jobs on the ground, to fuel them and get them on their way. At times rapid refueling does get intense, we still had mortars that would hit close to the fuel farm, and when the gigantic helicopters like a Chinook or a Sea Stallion would approach it brought hurricane strong winds from the rotor wash. Once they landed and the dust cleared two fuelers would approach the helicopter. One Soldier would hook up the grounding equipment and the other would hook up the fuel nozzle. Then they would signal back to the fuel truck to begin the flow of fuel. As you crouch under the blades if you look up you can see all the static electricity from the helicopter blades, its actually very pretty to look at, a lot of different colors.

That was my job in a nut shell, I never got bored fueling aircraft, I took a lot of pride in what we did. All together we pumped two million gallons of fuel that deployment, we were pumping gas, kicking ass.

When we weren't fueling aircraft, we had a nice shack to lay around in, and unlike Macedonia, we had plenty of food and water, we didn't have to ration. We had so many girl scout cookies, muffins and Gatorade's we didn't know what to do with ourselves. But Soldiers being Soldiers we came up with a few ideas for the muffins at least. One of my Soldiers was named PVT Erkel, he was a younger, black, slender kid who wore glasses, he was a truck driver in the civilian world and he loved heavier set white women, and was a blast to have around. We made bets that PVT Erkel couldn't eat seven muffins, with no water in under two minutes, we all threw in five dollars. So, if he did it, the money was his, he only made it to three. The next Soldierly bet we made with Erkel, is that he had to swallow a whole large bottle of tobacco sauce in order two minutes. He was successful at that, but later he had to go to sick call. Another one of my Soldiers was SPC Husker from Nebraska, and one of my basketball buddies, and everything to him was a competition. Him and I bet on everything. We played poker, Tiger Woods golf, we even built a golf course on the FARP, it was the roughest nine holes I have ever played but it worked. He won't admit it, but I pretty much beat him at everything. I had some great guys and girls in my platoon, we kicked butt at our job, and we managed to not have to much drama.

Something did happen to me I didn't think was possible during war time. One of the other guys and I were leaving our morning shit from C Co Medevac, we had a HUMMV, and it had rained the night before. On our way back there were some nice puddles, the speed limit on post was like fifteen miles per hour. I was driving, and I looked over at SPC Boise, and said should I do it?

He replied, "hell yes Sarge." So I floored and we hit that puddle hard, and the next thing I knew a damn Military Police was pulling me over. He said he clocked me at forty five miles per hour when I hit the puddle. He wrote me an eleven-point ticket, and I wasn't allowed to drive on post anymore. I had to tell my SGM (Sergeant Major), and give classes to everyone in the company on the rules of driving on post. I couldn't believe it, I thought it was comical, I can see the headlines, 'Soldier loses driver's license during war'.

The deployment was coming to an end, and I was ready to get home. I felt very proud of all the fueling we accomplished that helped support the war efforts. Unfortunately, going back home in some ways was worse than being at war.

THE SEVENTH FLOOR

After leaving Iraq, I went to a military school to attend a Non Commission Officer (NCO) class for a promotion, I was there for two weeks, and going straight from Iraq into a school like that was tiring, but nonetheless I graduated, along with six others that were with me from Iraq. Following that school, it was time to head back home once again.

It was the first time I had a drink in about a year, and I was thirsty. The moment the guys and I hit the airport it was drinking time. The entire flight back I drowned myself in shots and beer. Finally back home, it felt good, I grabbed my duffle bags, stumbled to a taxi, and asked the driver he could stop by a grocery store about a mile from house so I could get some fresh milk, that's all I wanted. When we arrived he said he wouldn't wait for me, I was in no position to argue, he didn't speak very fluent English. Therefore, I took my duffle bags threw them in a grocery cart, grabbed some milk, and pushed the grocery cart about a mile back to my house.

That walk was comforting, I was at peace. Eighteen months of being away from home, just finished a military school, and I get to see my son the following day, and to top it all off, the deployment helped me get out of debt and save a lot of money, there wasn't much I could worry about.

We were given time off after Iraq, so for thirty days, I spent a lot of time with MAS, trying to make up for time that I was away from him. I booked airline tickets down to Texas to see my dad and all my relatives for a few days and then after that we were to fly to Tennessee to see my brother, his wife, and my niece.

For the record, I have so much respect for mothers, and single parents. Traveling with a young child and being a parent and protector of a child by yourself is a significant amount of work and responsibility. So for all passengers that get annoyed with crying babies on a plane, stop bitching, put head phones on, or reflect on your life and remember you were once a crying child who annoyed people as well.

Between a diaper bag, stroller, car seat, snacks, his clothes, superman and batman, my little back-pack with a pair of boxers, pair of socks, and a pack of smokes, I was loaded down while we traveled, but we both managed, he was a trooper.

MAS was able to see his great grandfather, and his grandfather. It's one thing for kids to see grandparents, but its heartwarming, and very moving for MAS to see his great grandparents. Besides me letting MAS accidently stand in a fire ant pit, and letting him roll off the bed and hit the floor, which sounded like a bowling ball dropping, the trip to Texas was great. Next stop was Tennessee, but to get there we had a layover in Atlanta, and that's when I lost it.

Everything was going smooth, we boarded the plane and were buckled in.

The flight attendant chimed in over the speaker, "sorry for the inconvenience, we have a mechanical issue and all passengers will have to get off the plane for a brief moment." No biggie, we got off, and it was about thirty minutes before they let us back on.

Chime in number two, "I dearly apologize, but the maintenance problem is bigger than we expected, we will be switching planes, please exit the airplane and wait for further information." Okay, no problem, definitely don't want to fly on a broke plane, they were just looking after our safety.

A couple hours went by, I started to get frustrated, then I looked at the monitors and everything was canceled into Memphis due to severe weather, I fucking lost it. I starting thinking about the logistical nightmare it is to fly somewhere in the Army, and I didn't want to be in that situation, I just wanted everything to go smooth, and it wasn't.

I rushed to the counter, and said "please, re-route my son and I back home," I begged her. We were able to get on a plane ASAP and head back home.

I don't think I was mentally prepared to travel, I just wanted to be home in my comfort zone, just a quiet place, with no people, no loud noises, no long lines, no people bitching or talking, I just wanted home.

Following my failed attempt at traveling to see family, I was very content with just being home. Although my mind felt content, a lot was going through my head at the time, things such as; deployment money was running out, my mortgage, my expensive drinking budget, divorce was soon to be final, child support, my job, and everyday life, not to mention I was lonely, I thought to myself, there was less stress in Iraq. I was starting to fall apart mentally. I know the biggest thing I was stressing about was the house my ex and I purchased. We got caught in the 'Subprime Mortgage Crisis of 2008' from the house we purchased in 2004. Long story short, we were financed when we shouldn't have been financed, and the contract was ignored by the mortgage company. I couldn't afford the increasing interest, it was outrageous, so one day I moved my stuff out, and went through the next year and a half of hell. I had to foreclose, and file bankruptcy on a second mortgage. I wasn't proud about the whole situation, but I put myself in a hole I couldn't dig out of. Fortunately, our government does offer help for dumb honest mistakes, and they realized the impact the late 2000's mortgage crisis had on citizens.

I pushed forward as long as I could without breaking down, I continued to work and do what I needed to do to stay above water, I was going through the motions of being a dad to MAS, I wasn't me, I hated me, I wanted to kill myself.

Then after a year and a half of being depressed, drunk, a liar and emotional wreck I called my good friend and supervisor, Kdawg, and told her I will not be coming in to work, my words were something like, hey, I am not right in the head. I was already drunk at five in the morning.

I wanted help, and I knew if I didn't get help, I would be dead by the end of the day, I had it all planned out. Kdawg took me seriously and knew something was wrong, she made phone calls and was staying in constant contact with me. Not sure the exact events that morning, but I do remember driving and going to get myself a six pack, I stopped close by the house and saw the cops drive by looking for me, they never saw me. I slammed my six pack and headed home, several co-workers, a Chaplin, and a NCO who specialized in suicides, were there to greet me. I didn't put up a fight, I just wanted to go somewhere so I could sober up and be in a place that didn't allow me to manipulate them. So Kdawg took me to the VA (Veterans Hospital). They quickly admitted me onto the seventh floor.

Not sure what it was that brought me to this point. I continuously asked myself, am I weak minded? Is it deployments? Seeing death? Divorce? Bankruptcy? Drinking? I could go on and on, but at this point in my life I didn't know what made me this way. All I knew is that I was on the edge ready to step off and fall so I could be free of all anger, demons, and anguish within myself.

When I walked through that steel bolted door to the seventh floor it was an eye opener for me, and even though we weren't criminals, they didn't want us wandering off. No shoe laces were allowed, everyone wore booties, the walls were completely white with no pictures. The floor was cold, my room only had a small bed with white sheets, a night stand and an overhead light. There were other patients there who had been in multiple times for drugs and alcohol that were a lot worse off than I was. It made me think real hard, and realize I didn't want to get lost on the path of no return, I still had my health, and my will to live was getting stronger once again.

For three days I went through withdrawals. My blood pressure averaged 160/110, I was constantly sweating, and I couldn't sleep for crap. Finally on the fourth day I was normal, I slept well, I was feeling good about myself. I really needed those four days to reflect on everything and get my shit together and man up. I was using alcohol to manage my problems, and that is not the way to deal with life.

I saw a therapist that fourth day and she agreed to release me. Sometimes we just need to stop, slow down, and regroup, and that's what I did, and thanks to Kdawg for being my life long friend and caring enough to help me that morning.

The biggest thing I learned in there is that all humans are wired different. We all take our unique paths, we all react to pain and depression in different ways, some can deal with it themselves, others need help, and it doesn't make you any more weaker mentally or physically. If you know you are troubled in your head then ask for help. So for now, I was back on my feet, sober, and ready to deal with life.

GUARD LIFE

Following my stay on the seventh floor I was sent off to FT Lee, Virginia to attend a military school for two weeks, I breezed through the course. The course was to help me get promoted. On my return back to my Aviation Unit I was promoted to the rank of SSG (Staff Sergeant).

Not only was my military career looking up, my divorce was final, my bankruptcy and foreclosure was finally put to rest, and after all the stressing of going through the foreclosure, the mortgage company I was with made payments back to me for the next two years, they were forced by the Government to do so to minimize lawsuits.

All in all, life was leveling out, I moved into a nice townhome, I was dating several girls, not at once, or was I? MAS was growing up fast, he started Tae Kwon Do, he was so cute in his little white uniform, and he was a beast at it, and I was also staying busy at work. I did have one set back that was tremendous pain but didn't keep me down.

In the middle of the night I jumped up out of bed, I had an incredible pain on the left side of my head, I looked in the mirror and my left eye was drooping a bit. I began to freak out, I thought I was suffering from a stroke. In pain and almost blind in my left eye I drove to the emergency room. After shots to the stomach for pain, and pain killers that didn't work, a doctor finally figured out I was experiencing cluster headaches, also called suicide headaches. They are called suicide headaches because people who suffered from them would commit suicide due to the extreme pain, and these are not migraine headaches. Migraines in no way shape or form compare to cluster headaches. Cluster headaches are explained as 'the worst pain known to medical science'. After the diagnoses I was put on oxygen, and remarkably they went away. The headaches were sporadic for the next few months, I walked around with a oxygen tank everywhere I went. I was mid thirties and felt like I was eighty years old walking around with that oxygen tank, but I didn't care, the oxygen took that horrible pain away.

As my cluster headaches began to fade, my work load was picking up. The reason being was that after 9-11 the National Guard became a whole different animal. The Aviation Unit I was in always had one Company/ Unit deployed to the middle East, and they are still deploying to this day. Along with deployments we also stayed constantly on the go at home in Colorado doing mountain rescue missions, fighting fires, and helping in flood relief.

Before the Guard became so involved in the post 9-11 era, I viewed the Guard just like the men in the movie *Rambo*. In the movie guardsmen blow up a cave that Rambo (Sylvester Stallone) was in. One of the guardsmen asks the other to go check out the cave. The guardsmen says, "I only do this shit one weekend a month, I ain't going in after him". Another perception I had of the Guard is from when I was in Germany I saw a National Guard unit at the chow hall, They were in there for three weeks doing some training. They looked rough; uniforms were out of regulations, hair was long, a lot of lower ranking Soldiers looked to be fifty years old or more, so as active duty Soldiers we made fun of them, but I never realized I would become one of them a couple of years down the road.

Although the National Guard may look out of regulations or a little over weight, old, or beat up, it's because most guardsmen are already veterans, and have been there and done that. Unlike active duty where Soldiers stay in a one place for a short period of time and then move on to somewhere new, guardsmen will be in the same unit for multiple years and in-turn become masters at their job position. All in all, both active military, guard and reserves, all have the same goal, to keep the citizens of the United States safe.

Following my promotion to SSG I worked right under my Platoon Sergeant, SFC DT. We made a great team. He dealt with all the higher up people, he had that calmness, and patience to deal with the political crap from officers and higher ranking NCO's. He was our buffer between the platoon and the management, and he did a great job at it. With him being the go between I was able to manage the Soldiers and make missions happen without any interference.

We used to kick ass. During the fire season our helicopters would be deployed to drop water from the air. My platoon would drive fuel trucks to their location to help expedite the fuel process so they could drop more water and a faster rate.

Many times I took my platoon and fuel trucks all over the state to help fight fires, and we accomplished every mission. I loved my Soldiers, they respected me, and I respected them, but sometimes I was to nice and they got out of hand. Unfortunately, when they got out of hand, I had to become their leader and not their friend.

For instance, we had to go to a two week training area in southeast Colorado. The whole battalion was going. Instead of driving my fuel trucks at four in the morning to the training area, myself, SFC DT, and the platoon went down a day early. We set up our tents and the fuel area for when the helicopters came in the following day. Since it was just us fuelers, I brought some vodka and some pulled pork to surprise them. After we were all set up and ready to go, I invited them over to my tent and said, thanks for all your hard work, now lets drink. Needless to say, they were happy campers, and happy Soldiers take care of their leaders.

We had some drinks and great food, and I quickly went to my cot and fell asleep. Then at one thirteen in the morning, my head pops up out of my sleeping bag, and I faintly hear two voices yelling like they are on a roller coaster. I could hear the Gator(ATV, 4 wheeler with six tires) they were in. They were hammered driving the gator in the middle of a field raising hell. I shot up out of my cot, wearing nothing but my boxers, I put my sneakers on with no socks and ran toward the headlights on the gator, I was pissed. As I was running they did a big circle and headed back to our tents, I quickly stopped, turned around and started running back to the tents to chew their ass. While doing so I stepped in a hole and slammed down into a cactus bed. My adrenaline allowed me to jump up from the cactus, I had needles everywhere on me, I mean everywhere. I limped back to the tents. The two Soldiers that were fucking off in the gator were there, I walked up to the one driving, and without a word I grabbed him by the front collar, I lifted him off his legs and slammed him to the ground, my words were calm and simple, don't ever disrespect me again. As I disciplined the Soldier with force, I remember SPC Big Pimpin' in the background yelling, dammmnnnn SGT Reed just WWF'ed body slammed his ass, OHHH SHIIITTT Mutha Fucka. I think I got my point across. I wasn't mad, I was disappointed they disrespected me after I hooked them up with food and drinks. After the huge wrestling move I made, I sat in a chair in the pitch black and started picking my cactus out of my legs. My guys joined in with flashlights and helped me pluck for about an hour or so. Even after plucking all those needles that night, I ended up still plucking needles two weeks later. Stay away from drunk Soldiers and cactus, that's the only advice I can give you.

I always wanted my Soldiers to have fun, and know that I would do anything for them. In return I expected them to take care of me as a leader, and execute every mission flawlessly, and that they did.

A couple of days before we were to leave our training area, one of our Chinooks got called up to assist in a mountain rescue. It was a routine mission, our pilots were highly trained for rescues. But this time was different, the Chinook blades hit the back of a mountain and they had to make a hard landing at about 12000 feet. The crew luckily walked away with minor injuries.

I was asked to do something that's never been done before, I had to defuel the aircraft at twelve thousand feet by hand. Two of the biggest obstacles were not spilling any fuel on the ground. There was a water source nearby we didn't want to spill fuel in it, the number one priority was to protect the environment. The other obstacle was listening to officers tell me how to do my job. In the civilian world, imagine a manager telling a professional cook how to make eggs. Basically, I listened to them but did it my way anyways. Sure enough, we were successful. We used manual pumps and defueled around six hundred gallons of fuel in to fifty five gallons drums and moved the drum by hand through rugged terrain into a connex and then a Blackhawk slung loaded the fuel down to the bottom of the mountain. It was flawless, we did what we needed to do with no spills, and no injuries.

My fuelers and I supported a lot of fires as well, we were always there ready to pump gas, granted there is a lot of unnecessary politics involved, but at the end of the day, I didn't give a shit about politics, officers, or higher up telling me how to do things. My number one priority was always to get fuel to aircraft so they can save lives, property and animals.

We supported several fires every summer, but the end of summer 2013, it wasn't fires, it was floods that devastated the state. Many of families and wildlife were affected, once again we were called upon to do rapid refueling for helicopters doing rescues. We quickly deployed, and we pumped thousands of gallons of fuel. Rescues were delayed until the fuelers arrived, without us the aircraft had to go to a local airport, shut down the engines and then fuel up. With us being there on sight to rapid refuel, aircraft were able to make a faster turnaround, and the end results were rescuing more families, and animals. It's a great feeling knowing we could make a difference, yes the air crews do amazing things, but they can't do it without support. Sometimes I looked at being a fueler as like a lineman in the NFL. Lineman block and make it possible for a running back to gain yards; fuelers, cooks, mechanics, medics, and all support Soldiers are lineman, we make it possible for infantry, air crew, special ops, tankers, field artillery, and other combat arms to go and execute their mission and gain ground against the enemy.

The National Guard always had something going on if it were here at home or overseas. Sadly, being part of the military, one thing you will see for sure is death.

Our Chinook unit was in Afghanistan during 2011. August 6th 2011, one of our Aviation Chinooks were shot down in Iraq, the Chinook was carrying Seal team Six, the same team that killed Osama Bin Laden. Genuine D, one of the most genuine, respectful, pilot/warrant officer I would ever meet was piloting the chinook. A Rocket Propelled Grenade took down the Chinook and killed everyone on board. Extortion 17 was the call sign, they were gone, it was the biggest loss so far in the Afghan war. God bless Extortion 17 and their families.

Genuine D and I worked hand in hand for years, he was our safety officer at our Aviation building, and I was the environmental/fueler/

recycle/HAZMAT guy at our hangar. He was very easy to work with, and he listened, but he did something every day that bothered me. I probably passed Genuine D several times throughout the day, and he was always walking with a purpose, but in the afternoons when he would walk by me he would always say good gorning, as I passed him of course I thought to myself, what the fuck Genuine D, its two in the afternoon and you are saying good morning, I just laughed within myself, I missed that. It was a huge loss.

Genuine D's funeral was breath taking. For almost one hundred miles along the highways, first responders were lined up on bridges flying American flags, and at the funeral, our helicopters did a fly over that put tears to your eyes, he was gone, but his kindness and heart will always be with me. He was a stellar man, father, friend, and pilot for our country.

The following year, our Chinooks guys returned home with an emotional ceremony, It was tough not having all the Soldiers return from war, I had another loss in my life that hit me hard.

Remember my good friends F2 and LLF from Germany? They went on a cruise to the Bahamas. Tragedy struck one evening, F2 had fallen overboard, and after thirty hours of search and rescue attempts he was never found. I cannot imagine what she went through on that ship. F2 attended my first wedding, and we had made so many memories together. They were such a hoot to be around. LLF's mom from Nuremberg calls me fucckkkeee, because back when I was in Germany and we would go to her mom's house I said the word fuck a lot, so naturally, they call me fuckee. I will never forget the time I served with F2, and LLF I love you, always, you will forever be my friend.

My timeline might be off from 2008 through 2013, but this was a time in my life when I was really starting to grow and mature. I was in my mid-thirties, I was becoming a leader in the guard, MAS was growing like a weed, I actually went back to college, to continue my thirty year associates degree. Not to disregard the passing of Genuine D and F2, but I was managing life well or so I thought, I was still drinking and smoking, but little did I know I was about to meet someone that changed my life forever.

MBW

Sometime during 2012, my unit was at the qualifications range for our M16 rifles. We all stayed in barracks, male and females on the same floor but separated by rooms. DT, myself and another NCO were walking down the hallway and saw one of the Soldiers in her room brushing her long blonde hair. I took notice of it, and was instantly attracted. She was a lot younger, and also I out ranked her, but she wasn't directly under me, and she was not in my platoon. According to Army regulations I was not doing anything wrong or illegal if I were to pursue her.

The long weekend ended and I was back home in my townhome on a Sunday evening, and what does a thirty something single guy do now days? Yep! You guessed it, I searched Facebook for her and sent her a friend request.

It wasn't long, I believe that same night she accepted my friend request. I was beyond excited. I started small talk with her, and told her I was going to come see her at work the following weekend. MAS and I drove to the Target she worked at a little over an hour away. The town smelled like cow shit constantly, but it's a nice college town, and I'm sure you get used to the smell at some point. I don't think she thought we would come visit her but we did. I bought MAS a toy for the inconvenient ride, you know how kids are. She was working at the Starbucks inside Target. So naturally I went an ordered a chocolate banana smoothie. As she started to make it she said, we don't have bananas, I immediately thought to myself, there is a whole shit load of them in the produce section, it's a Super Target. But I just went along with it. She made it, and charged me like almost seven dollars. We said bye, and I took a sip, that was the most bland smoothie I have ever had. It was disgusting. I tossed it in the trash. There went seven dollars down the drain. Beside the smoothie she ripped me off with, it was a successful trip, I think she was impressed that I traveled all that way to see her.

One thing led to another, and before I knew it, we were actually dating, I hadn't dated in years, I forgot what it was like. I fell for her, she didn't give me any crap, and was so easy to get along with, I was finally happy again. We would run together in the mornings, and hang out in the evenings, it was nice to have someone that I could get along with, and who was willing to put up with me.

The only thing I was worried about was her age. I was fourteen years older than her, so I wasn't sure how her maturity level would be, but then I thought about it. I was thirty six and still not mature, so I figured we would be just fine. It helped that she was actually really grown up for her age and had a good head on her shoulders, and she was smarter than I was. This was finally the girl I was going to spend the rest of my life with, but in order to do that, I knew I had to work on myself to keep this relationship alive.

The biggest thing I had to do to keep the relationship alive was to quit smoking, not just for her, but for myself and MAS. After twenty two years of smoking cigarettes I began the journey to quit. I reached the point where I would only smoke when I drank, which was every evening. The other part of the day I would tire my jaw out from nicotine gum and chewing tobacco. I also had a patch on my shoulder for extra measure, I was a wired nicotine machine, my heart was popping like a popcorn machine. I was able to kick the patch phase, now it was nicotine gum, chew, and smokes when I drank. Kicking the nasty chew habit was next.

While at work, MBW decided to stop by my work without letting me know, and I was out fueling helicopters, and just like I always do, I left my Copenhagen chew on my desk. She didn't know I chewed. When I came back in my office, a nasty note laid next to my chew, it read what the fuck is this? I couldn't hide it anymore, I sucked it up, apologized, and that was it for chewing. It's a disgusting habit anyways, spit everywhere, breath stinks, black shit in between your teeth, its just not attractive at all. Lastly, cigarettes had to go before the nicotine gum. After a year or so, I was done smoking,

I learned to hate cigarettes, they smell, they are expensive, they gave me anxiety, they make you look old, and I had to freeze my ass off outside when I wanted to smoke. It just wasn't for me anymore. I hear people say that they like smoking, and the doctor tells them they are healthy, that is what you call denial. I don't judge smokers, it's an awful addiction, it's hard to get off those damn things. I will say this, I am very addictive person, and I enjoyed smoking, it was part of me, if I can quit, anyone can, you just have to want to. I wasn't out of the woods yet, that damn nicotine gum sucks as well, it was hard to ditch those damn things. The way I ended the nicotine gum was that I didn't have a choice. My jaw hurt so bad, MBW wouldn't kiss me and I was tired of shoveling money towards them, so that was it, I was done, nicotine free, and will never touch it again.

Although it was my own decision to smoke all those years ago, it was a huge accomplishment in my life to quit. MAS and MBW loved it so much that I was done with that nasty addiction, and it was refreshing seeing their reaction and positivity to me quitting. No more going outside during restaurant visits, no more waiting in the car for them while I smoked, and the best of all, I had extra money to spend on us.

That was a huge plus for me. I gained some points with MBW, MAS said I smelled great; I had no smoke smell, great smelling axe spray, and cheap after shave, clothes were Tide fresh, I was clean. That part of my life was history, and I was proud of it.

Continuing on, MBW and I were getting to close, so close that the question was dwindling in my head, should I ask her? Well we will see what happens, but for now, we were rolling right along.

After numerous times of being with MBW, the day came that I had to tell my ex-wife, that MBW was a good person and treated MAS awesome. It is hard for divorced parents to have your child with your ex's boyfriend or girlfriend. Not to mention, its harder on the child. But thankfully, everything worked out, X-Wife trusted me, and trusted MBW.

MAS and MBW are both hard headed, and sarcastic, crap talking step mom to step son. They always use me to talk to each other, I have to force them to talk to each other. Bottom line, they are in each other's lives, and they have never said it, but I know damn well they love one another. They just don't admit it, but they are good, which makes me more than happy! That's all I need.

With the lack smoke, and the anxiety lessened of hoping those two got along, I couldn't ask for anymore. They honestly were my heros, and my life, I needed them both.

Then the day came, it was late summer, we took an evening walk to a nearby park. The mood was perfect; soft, dark green grass, no wind in the air, the sun was half way silhouetted behind the Rocky Mountains, the suns remaining light turned the clouds a florescent orange color that blended with the darkening blue sky, we laid on our stomachs and talked.

After a few minutes passed by, I nonchalantly said to her, "oh here is your set of keys for the truck." I had bought a brand new Nissan Frontier the day before.

Earlier, before we left the house I had put a ring on the set of keys, that's how I was going to ask her to marry me.

She took the keys, and replied "ah thanks babe," and just placed them on the grass in front of her. Instantly I thought to myself, WTF, SMH, OMG, pick up the damn keys and look at them.

So finally I said, "would you look at the damn keys?" With a smile on her face, and a tear brewing in her beautiful eyes, she whispered it, yes. That was that, we were getting married.

By this time I had moved out of the townhome I was in, and moved into a buddy's house that I worked with, the timing was perfect. He was leaving for a year on a deployment to the middle east so he let me stay at his house for year rent free, all he wanted is for me to take care of his place, and respectfully I did.

MBW moved in with me, and the best part of it all, was that since we didn't have to pay rent, we were able to plan and pay off the wedding and the rings. So when the wedding came in a year or so we wouldn't have to worry about any debt. The timing of everything was perfect.

Along with the road to a wedding, I began coaching MAS's lacrosse team. I will be the first to admit, I didn't know a damn thing about lacrosse. Before the first practice I did a lot of research online, and was able to get the basics down and felt confident about conducting practices. As I looked more and more into lacrosse, I quickly realized it is very similar to basketball, just with sticks, but the concept is the same; move the ball around, pass and cut, set picks, give and goes, constant running, man to man defense or zone. Since I have been a life long basketball fan, I coached lacrosse like I coached basketball. It took a few games to get in a rhythm, but as long as the coach and your kids are having fun, and parents keep their mouth's shut, youth sports can make life long memories.

Our lacrosse season started off in the slumps, we found ourselves with an 0-4 losing record. The boys were tired of losing, I was tired of losing, but I wasn't going to let the start of the season determine who we were as a team. We had a game thirty minutes away. The boys and I were determined to get this win, I bought them Krispy Cream Donuts to boost their motivation, and sure enough, it finally happened, we were victors. The sad thing was that the team we played hadn't won a game yet either, I felt for the coach, I felt his pain, and he was a great sport about it. After we got that first win, motivation and confidence sky rocketed, weekend after weekend we were winning, and having fun doing it. The end of the season approached, and we had a state tournament weekend at Dicks Sporting Goods field. It was a great event, people were tailgating, small tents were spread out selling lacrosse attire, food stands everywhere, it was like a professional game was being played, it was big deal for my team. Sadly, I went in to the tournament with a negative attitude, I had the runts of the league, the bad news bears of lacrosse, or kids that had never touch a lacrosse stick. What I did have, was determined, motivated kids who loved having fun playing on the team, and heart, I had a great group of boys.

We went into the tournament as the lowest seed. Therefore, our first game was against a high ranking team, and miraculously we beat them, I honestly cant remember the details, but is all I know is that we won.

The weather became cold and rainy, great weather for lacrosse. We kept winning, each time the brackets got smaller, my boys were tired, I was tired. But we did it, we made it to the championship game which was to be played about seven that night.

I gathered the boys, gave them a motivational speech, and we headed to the field. On the way to the field, I was walking behind one of my players and he was limping bad, I asked him if he was okay.

He said, "yes coach, I am good."

"Well why you limping C-Dawwgg?" I asked.

He responded, "I am not hurt coach, my balls are sticking to my leg."
I started laughing so hard, and the team laughed as well, we went into

that final game laughing and having fun. Kids are great, and say some silly stuff sometimes.

To make a long game short, we were down five to four with about nineteen seconds left, we gained possession of the ball and I quickly called a timeout and set a play up. Very simple play, pass it to my speedy kid and have him go down and shoot. It was executed flawlessly, and he went to shoot on goal and missed by inches, we lost by one. Some boys were in tears, it was a tough loss, but we started as nothing, and became so much more, I was proud of them. I hope they grow up and remember what it took for our team to be successful; teamwork, positive attitude, motivation, passion, and fun. I loved that team. The following year we actually won the championship, I had a couple different kids on the team, and not sure why, but I didn't feel the same about that team as I had the season before.

I coached for a few more years, but as the kids got older, it wasn't fun for me anymore. I was drinking before games, taking shots in porta potties in-between quarters, I also getting kicked out of games, for arguing with opposing team parents, because every game was the world championship to them. I just wasn't having fun anymore, and it wasn't the kids, it was the parents and the league that strayed me from coaching. All in all, I will never forget the kids I coached, I hope I made a small impact on their life, just like mine made on me in youth sports.

Coaching became a hobby for me. It's honestly my next dream after writing a book to coach college basketball, but who knows! Football season came around, so I had time off, and also it was time for the big wedding.

August 30th, 2013 was our wedding day. I wasn't nervous. I was content, I knew MBW was great for me, and she treated me right. Only close friends and family came to the wedding, it was small but special. MBW was astonishing as she walked down the stairs to the song "A Moment Like This" by Kelly Clarkson. The night was perfect. There was one thing that made MBW upset, MAS was still young, and didn't want to leave my side, so I let him sleep on a couch in the honey moon suite with us. I knew eventually MBW would get over being mad, but it took a year or so, ooppsss!!!

As my career was coming to an end, and she was just starting hers, we were able to purchase a nice townhome. We bought at the right time, because as soon as our state legalized marijuana, property values sky rocketed.

MBW worked full time for the National Guard Honor Guard, she would perform funerals for Veterans and do the colorguards for sporting events, she also was determined to finish her associates degree and become a veterinary technician. She loved animals, she started school to become a nurse but didn't like that people talked back and can be rude, so she decided to spend her life helping our furry friends, and she is amazing at it.

After two years of hard studying she finished school, quickly quit the Honor Guard, and accepted a job as a veterinary technician, I was proud of her, for the simple fact that being a full-time National Guard Soldier pays good money, but to her it wasn't about the money. It was about doing what she loved, and being happy with her career.

I was a lucky dad and husband. MAS was excelling at school and sports, MBW launched her career, we were home owners, and for the first time I can remember my life was stable, I couldn't ask for more. I had two of the greatest people behind me who supported me.

Than it happened again, my unit got called up to deploy again to Kuwait, with rumors of going back into Iraq. This was my last time, I was to get myself mentally prepared, and just make it through the next year.

I AM DONE

It was December 2015, our physical training to prepare for our deployment was to begin in February, but in actuality it started in December with the planning. The part of being over in Kuwait or Iraq and doing my mission wasn't an issue, it was the politics and people I had to deal with, and I am not talking about my Soldiers. So unfortunately just the thought of going through with this deployment aided in sending me to the emergency room twice in a two week span. There might have been many things to contribute to my emergency room visits, but the notification of this deployment put the icing on the cake.

The first time I went to the emergency room, MAS and I had tickets to the Miami Dolphins and Denver Bronco game. We were excited, got all dressed up in our Dolphins attire, and started driving to the football stadium. Not even before we got out of the neighborhood it hit me. My mind started rolling a hundred miles a minute, my heart pounded, worst of all I couldn't get a deep breath in. I gagged with each breath, struggling to get a breath in, throwing up in between breaths, I was suffering from a panic attack. Its one of the worst feelings to deal with. I have suffered from anxiety for the past twenty years, but it was never treated up until a couple of years before, I just dealt with it. I was taking medication for my anxiety, but it wasn't helping at all, whatever it was that triggered my panic attacks, if it were thoughts of deploying again, leaving MAS and MBW, the politics of a deployment, I couldn't pin point it. I had a thousand thoughts of worry, all bouncing around in my little brain. MAS and MBW took

120

me to the emergency room and I was able to get calmed down, and was good for the night.

The following day I had to take MAS across town to go to school. Once again my mind started racing, I stopped ten cars back at a stop light, and it started again, short of breath, heart racing, and my head in a thousand places, I turned the truck around and went back home, I just couldn't physically or mentally drive him to school. Luckily, that afternoon I had an appointment with my doctor, and it was as simple as upping the dose of anxiety medicine. Like I mentioned earlier, I have dealt with anxiety for years; throwing up in the mornings because my mind would move faster than my breathing, I would think to much. I would think of the unknown. I would think of what could happen. I would think of failure. I would anticipate what people would say. I would think of the negative side to everything. Before coaching my sons games I remember walking away, hide and struggle to catch my breath, but ended up throwing up every time. I hated it, it sucked, and I can't explain why I suffer from anxiety, and it's miserable. Unless you suffer from it, you have no idea what it is like.

I hear comments a lot when a celebrity, or someone of significant importance suffers from anxiety or depression, the first words out of fans mouth's are, they make millions, what the fuck they have to worry about? and the first thought to myself was, shut the fuck up. Anxiety doesn't know how much money you have, how much fame you have, how poor you are, how successful you are, or how much everyone thinks that you are mentally stable. Prime examples are NBA Player, Kevin Love, and Model, Gisele Bundchen, it's a mental health disorder that is challenging to live with.

Nonetheless, I had to continue on, I had to get mentally prepared for this last deployment. My good friend and Platoon Sergeant SFC DT retired. His retirement bumped me up to his position, I was now the Platoon Sergeant, so I needed to be mentally strong for all my Soldiers. Yes, I could have gotten out of the deployment for medical issues, but I needed to be there for my Soldiers. I needed to be that buffer between the higher up leadership and my troops.

As training begin I wasn't happy with how the company I was in went about everything. I have deployed with this company in 2006, have done many state fire and flood missions, and we were very successful. Our main mission was to support our Aviation helicopters, we had three different platoons, they were the fuelers, the cooks, and ground maintenance mechanics, basically we were the support company for the Battalion. But this time it just didn't feel right.

My main focus was to protect my Soldiers, and take care of them, by supplying them with food, water, a bunk, correct pay, and proper counseling to make it through the year. It just seemed like I always had to fight for those things through higher up. This is the point when I started losing faith in the National Guard, and this deployment determined that after twenty two years I would retire on my return home. It wasn't for me anymore.

During the previous year we were down south training, we were there for the weekend to qualify with our M16's once again. The day was long, two of the Soldiers in my platoon just could not qualify, they couldn't shoot targets at all. They were just a bad shot, but that didn't frustrate me as a leader. That is what we go and try to qualify for, to see if you can shoot your weapon, and get the practice. Unfortunately, leadership all the way from my Company to the Battalion Commander did not see it that way. So the two Soldiers in my platoon that could not shoot to save their lives, my leadership decided to have two other Soldiers lie next to them and shoot down their targets so it can look good on paperwork that the whole Battalion qualified their machine gun 100% during the qualification range. I did not know that this took place until on the way back to our home military base when I asked if everyone had qualified, and they said yes, if you count the extra targets we shot down because we were ordered to do so. I was pissed, I couldn't believe it, but I was hated by leadership because I always stood up to them.

By all means, I am no saint, and I have done stupid shit in my life, but I would never sacrifice Soldiers life by sticking a Soldier who is weak at shooting as a gunner or rifleman on a patrol. We all have strong and weak points, if someone can't shoot, they might be amazing on the radio, or a great pilot, great cook, great mechanic, or a great computer whiz. Same at the office in civilian world, you might have someone great at typing reports, but is terrible at communicating. Therefore, you have them type all your stuff, and keep them away from the phone. Bottom line would you want someone fighting next to you that is not comfortable on that weapon system? It just appears like they are all because some officer/manager wanted their evaluation report to look good of 100% Soldiers qualified on the M16/machine gun range? By the way, no company in the military has ever had a 100% first time go on a range, unless you are FOS troopers from star wars, they hit everything.

The sickening part about the whole thing, is the Sunday we got home we had a family day and the Battalion Commander spoke to all the families and said, Your loved ones did a great job, blah blah blah blah, this is the first time any unit has ever accomplished 100% on a weapons range, the families clapped. I wanted so bad to open my mouth and say you are full of shit, but I had to keep it cool. The thought went through my head of these assholes taking my guys and shooting down targets of others who just can't shoot to make the leadership feel good about themselves.

Along with pencil whipping weapons qualification ranges, there was an incident where a loud mouth Soldier would come into work at the Honor guard and call my wife 'Sweet Tits' every morning. It didn't bother MBW to much, but when it happens all the time it gets old, and it bothered other co-workers of hers, and it bothered me. The Soldier was fired from the Honor Guard, and a couple of years later he was put in my platoon without leadership having any knowledge that he was fired for sexual harassment against my wife. I quickly told the chain of command, and they removed him from my platoon. I called down to the state Equal Opportunity Officer and she had no record of any incident of him being fired for sexual harassment, again I was losing more and more faith in the system.

While I was deployed in the middle east a married male Lieutenant had an affair with a lower enlisted female Soldier, and this is just one incidents of affairs that go on in the military, they happen constantly. For example the General that was accused of adultery that we all heard about in the news. Most of it gets swept under the carpet, just like most illegal issues, because God forbid if a Commander has a bad report of sexual misconduct within his Battalion or Company. These are only a few things, I could write a whole other book on all the misconduct and abuse by people in power in the Army, but I am not going to do that. Not all Soldiers are bad, there are still some honorable men and women who take pride in wearing the uniform, and who live by the Army Values.

One morning I was on the treadmill at work, and there was a officer running next to me, we had the morning news on. The report was of an NFL player who had been arrested for drinking and driving. The officer made the comment, NFL Players are a bunch of thugs, I responded with damn sounds like the military, we have a crap load of drinking and driving arrests and deaths from alcohol, so is the Army a bunch of THUGS?. Needless to say he didn't have an answer to that.

All in all, after twenty plus years in the military, I was just getting fed up with a lot of things, I started to get very short tempered and could tell I couldn't do this to much longer.

It was inevitable, I was deploying regardless, and the time came to say good bye to MAS once again. He was a tough kid, I have missed birthdays, sporting events, and have always had to play catch-up when I returned home. But he understood, he knew it was my job, and always supported me. I wrote him a letter before I left, that he carries with him on a daily basis.

We took a flight down to Ft Hood, Texas for training again. The training wasn't so bad, my platoon did a lot of fueling and everything was going smooth. Then it was time for the long dreaded flight to the Middle East once again. We stopped in Germany for a couple of days. Our Commander said we could have some drinks, I didn't hesitate, I was the first one to buy a German beer out of about one hundred and fifty Soldiers. We drank until early morning and then loaded buses to go to a German farm where they served us smoked lamb, chicken and sausage, it was delicious. Half the Soldiers, including myself, then passed out on the lawn due to jet lag and drinking all night. The other half of us got hammered at the German BBQ. When was all said and done, pretty much the flight into Kuwait sucked. The majority of us were hungover, both from drinking and jet lag.

We made it to Kuwait, we found out that we were permanent party at the camp. Kuwait is not bad at all, but of course we still had people that bitched and complained. The camp had bingo Wednesday night, poker games throughout the week, a movie theatre, a state of the art gym, with cycling and yoga classes, a great chow hall, basketball, ping pong, pool, darts, softball, basically it was a resort for the next six months. My platoon had our mission, and it wasn't fueling aircraft, contractors took over fueling operations, we also had contractors that cooked our food, did our laundry, cleaned our bathrooms, and other duties that us as Soldiers should be doing, but let's go ahead and pay contractors a crap load of money to do a job that we should be doing.

Moving on, I ended up having almost fifty joes under me, both National Guard and active duty. Our job was to turn on and off generator lights throughout the camp. We were also in charge of transporting Soldiers throughout Kuwait, including to the airport, I also had a small group in charge of flight line security, and lastly we had several other small duties we would have to fulfill from time to time.

Nonetheless, we stayed busy, but the thing that irritated me the most is that it wasn't good enough for leadership. We just spent nearly six months in the states training up to spend six months in Kuwait, now they wanted to train more. I did not agree with this at all. The way I saw it, is that although it was a laid back deployment our job was to maintain a camp in Kuwait so that other units 'actually' going into Iraq and Afghanistan could stop through for a week or so and then move on to combat operations up north. Once again I was fed up, I just wanted to do our duties assigned to us, and then go home, but we had to do repetitive training, so that once again a Commander and 1SG could have great evaluation reports. To sum it up, we trained at FT Hood, Texas to come to Kuwait to do a job, we didn't train at Ft Hood, Texas to train in Kuwait. Once again, I just had to suck it up, I wasn't the one in charge, so I tried my hardest to keep my mouth shut, but sometimes that is a very difficult task for me.

Time went by, and the deployment was over half way over, and then I got a message from MBW that her National Guard Unit was set to deploy. I just took a deep breath in, and said, I am so fucking done with this shit.

I am in Kuwait dealing with a deployment that I thought was useless, and my wife is about to start training up to deploy to Iraq.

With the news I received about MBW deploying, I struggled to stay focused, but nonetheless, I pulled through it. I just kept getting more and more irritable at the military as days went by.

As it grew closer to flying home, there was something that bothered me bad that made my final decision, that when I get home, I will retire.

We had an Indonesian man that cleaned our bathrooms every day, I thanked him each and every morning. He dealt with a bunch of dirty, disrespectful assholes that would shower, shit, shave, and leave the bathroom a mess. It was disgusting the way some Soldiers cannot clean up after themselves. The military to me just wasn't the same anymore, discipline was a thing of the past. Before I left, I bought the Indonesian two packs of cigarettes, and gave him a Battalion coin to thank him for his hard work every day, he had a tear in his eye and hugged me. I hated seeing people that come from third world countries to support us Americans, and they see how undisciplined and childish we can be. It was extremely embarrassing to me.

Don't get me wrong, I am again not talking about all Soldiers, but I have seen the discipline become non-existent over twenty years, and maybe its just me, but the Army needs to get back to the basic fundamentals. Blah blah blah blah, I am done rambling on about that.

The deployment was coming to an end, despite all my built up frustration, I managed to keep my cool, well kind of! Eventually I made it home, and it was a great feeling, I had roughly four months until I could retire and never put the Army uniform on again.

CRUISING ALONG

December 2016 I was home. January 2017 my wife and I took our first cruise ever, we had to fit in vacation before she started training. We flew down to Houston and my cousins picked us up and took us to Galveston where our cruise ship was set to disembark from.

The cruise was amazing, I loved everything about it. There are people from all over the world that work on cruise lines, and they are great people, they treat guests like royalty. Not only was the ship crew exceptional, but so were all the passengers, and just like the ship crew, the passengers were from all walks of life. There was no color, religion, or profiling on the ship, we were all there to enjoy the beautiful ocean, and countries we visited.

The only bad part about the cruise is I gained five pounds. Holy crap the food was fantastic, and it was free all day and all night, not to mention endless ice cream. The best part was I stood on the deck looking across the endless blue water and reflecting back on my life, and I took a moment to thank God for putting me there at that moment. I closed my eyes and breathed, listening to the ship cut through the waves as it sailed across the ocean, soaking up the warm sun, and hearing birds sing in the distance, I was once again at ease for the first time in a long time.

After a great week on the ocean, visiting Jamaica, The Cayman Islands and Cozumel, it was time to head back home and face the fact that my wife had to start her training. Although she wasn't set to actually leave until late summer, we didn't see each other that much because of the time spent training up for her deployment.

She had some downtime around April, and we decided to do another cruise, this time it was with my son, my brother and his wife, and my niece. We sailed to the Florida Keys, the Bahamas, and then back to Galveston. It was a great trip once again, MAS enjoyed playing basketball all day long, and I enjoyed losing a crap load of money at the casino.

It was hard to enjoy this cruise, the first cruise was celebrating my return home, this cruise was a vacation before MBW deployed, and she was going to far worse places then where I was at in Kuwait. But she pulled one more vacation off for me before she left, and bless her heart this is how it went down.

My fortieth birthday was right around the corner. She apparently had been planning this for months, saving money and hiding it from me. Then sent us on what I thought was a wild goose chase around town. I was kind of irritated to be going places I had no idea about until I came home and found out it was to get me out of the house so she could set up my surprise party.

My son and I were given an address and told to go there and enjoy ourselves. We pulled up to Luigi's and enjoyed a wonderful lunch, of course all paid for in advance. Once lunch was complete the waiter brought out a brown paper sack with our next location in it as well as a little memento. Inside the bag was an address and clue to the next place, which read that we will reach new heights and to go up, up and away. A set of Miami dolphins luggage tags were inside the bag.

Once we figured out the next location, and drove onward, we pulled up to a rock climbing gym. Turns out my father-in-law and brother-in-law were waiting for us there to help with the next part of our scavenger hunt. We were told in order to get the next clue we had to climb the wall. My fat ass had just eaten lunch and had a hard time getting up the wall. I sent my brother-in-law, to help me out. At the top of the wall was a Ryan Tannehill #17 jersey and another clue that told us we need to go relax and rejuvenate.

I was enjoying myself but was growing more irritated that I couldn't know anything. We drove back towards Aurora and ended up at a salon for a pedicure. This was the best place, my toes needed some tender loving care.

My son had never had a pedicure, so this was a pretty cool bonding experience for us, but I have to admit we got some pretty weird looks. Who cares? We sat there and enjoyed getting our feet lathered up and soaking in the warm water and jets. At the end of this stop we got a Miami Dolphins string backpack and the final clue telling us to head back home. We had honestly enjoyed our day and I was worn out, it takes a lot of work to be pampered.

I remember walking up to our house, the garage door was open and there was chairs and tables outside, people were hanging around having a drink, when everyone shouted HAPPY BIRTHDAY!!! I was in shock that all this was going on while we were running around town. I couldn't believe that on MBW's tiny break in between training she made this all about me and pulled this off. Come to find out the scavenger hunt wasn't even the best part of the day. The best part were tickets to a Dolphins game...in Miami, everything paid for, and a limo to pick my son and I up to take us to the airport, I was ecstatic. She is an incredible human, wife, step mom, animal lover and Soldier.

MAS and I did our trip to Miami, we had a memorable trip, everything was perfect, but the sad part is that MBW was gone, she had left to start her tour in the Middle East.

The only positive aspect of doing back to back deployments is the money. We were financially well off, but the separation we went through over two and a half years was taxing on our marriage. But at the end of the day she is the one I wanted to come home to, and I wanted her to come home to me. Sure, there were temptations to have an affair, and I am sure it crossed her mind, it's a natural thought when being away from your significant other for so long, but we are still with each other and happy, we both can't stand loud noises in our house from war and blowing shit up, but nonetheless we are happy.

I didn't want to hear or think about what she was going through in Turkey and Iraq, every now and then she would share stories of her field artillery missile launching truck blowing up ISIS and getting confirmed kills. She is a tough girl, and was excellent at doing combat arms, which women recently had been cleared to do. She was just as good as any other male on the battle field. I was so proud of her, I bragged about her to everyone.

Back home, I was on a routine while MBW was gone. I took as much time off as I could from work, I was getting ready to retire anyway, so I pretty much said screw everyday and found every excuse in the book to not be at work. Granted, it was hard enough focusing everyday at work when your wife is deployed in a predominantly male unit, I tried to keep my mind from wondering about what could be going on. Therefore, I went to the bar daily, it was automatic for me, I just didn't want to think about her being in Iraq, Turkey, and wherever else she might have been.

During her tour, I realized how hard it is to be the Army wife. Paying bills, dealing with everyday life, taking care of our pets, and numerous other chores that comes along with everyday life. Some people would say I am crazy by saying this, but I guarantee most Soldiers who have been deployed would agree. I always thought being on deployment was less stressful than being at home and dealing with the every day stress of long lines, traffic, rude people, paying bills, where the next meal is coming from, and the list goes on, being on deployment you don't have all those stressors.

There was one night I had to deal with a stressor of taking care of one of our pets, and it didn't go over smooth. I had mentioned to MBW over text that the cats and Scribbles (our Guinea pig), there claws were getting long. Being the great vet tech she is, she explained the easiest way to cut their nails. I was successful with the kitties, but Scribbles on the other hand, was a shit show to put it lightly.

The first step was pulling Scribbles out of her cage, it took a few grabs but I got her. She was a plump, black and white, mean ass Guinea Pig, with big toenails that needed chopped. As I held her against my chest, she shed like crazy all over me, I think she was scared to death of me. I held her tight and told my son to hand me the nail clippers. I clipped a couple with no issues, and then on the third toe, I clipped it and blood starting squirting everywhere, and she screamed in a high pitch that sounded like this, EEEEEEGGGHHHHFFFUUUCCCKKKK. I started to panic as blood poured all over the kitchen floor, I had to act fast, and that I did.

"Throw me the peanut butter", I demanded, he opened it and I covered Scribbles wound with Skippy creamy peanut butter, it seemed to stop the bleeding. I felt horrible, I put her back in her kennel, and as soon as I did she starting eating the peanut butter off her toe. As much as I wanted to care for her more, I figured she will be good, the blood should clot, hopefully. So I sat down and MAS asked me how she was doing, I calmly replied that she will be fine. Sure enough, her toe is still going strong to this day, peanut butter saved her life.

Every day was the same for me while she was gone, I wanted to make it through the day, and go to bed early so another day would be closer to her being home. I never understood what spouses go through emotionally during a deployment until I was on the other side of it. Therefore, I have so much respect for spouses who keep life going on the home front while their loved ones are deployed fighting to keep this country free.

For nearly three years we dealt with deployments, and it was finally over. Also my retirement ceremony was to be held right before her deployment ended. I tried to get her home early to be at my ceremony, but of course the National Guard wouldn't do that, but they will send high ranking officers home for weddings. Bottom line is they have sent people home for far less reasons, so this was another strike. I was pissed and done. I have served twenty two years all together in the military, both active duty and National Guard and I couldn't get my wife home a couple weeks early to celebrate my retirement.

As I did my retirement speech, I was hoping it would have been one of those stories you see on the news, and MBW would pop out of the crowd. But that shit didn't happen. Regardless, I gave a pretty good speech, my son was with me, and I gave him so much respect for the times I was away from him. I spoke my mind, but I didn't talk long, because I remember standing in long formations listening to someone speak and all I could think about was, shut the hell up, so I can go home. I kept my speech short, I am a Soldiers Soldier, I know what they been through all weekend and they were ready to go home. The following week and to this day I still hear my speech was epic from several people, not sure what I said, but I know for sure, I thanked my guys, and I know I said this, don't ever kiss anyone's ass, no man or woman on this earth is any better than you as a human being, we are all here to live, love, and die a happy life.

MBW never showed up as a surprise to my retirement ceremony, but I understood, she didn't want to leave her Soldiers in Turkey, she felt bad. I was initially upset she couldn't be there, but I got over it, she is a very loyal person.

July 8th, 2017, my birthday, my wife's unit returned from overseas, it was the perfect birthday present. I haven't held her in months, it was emotional, I was relieved she was home. We could finally get back to building our lives together.

Life got somewhat back to normal, but we both seemed off. Deep down I was struggling with retirement, and drinking a lot, and I couldn't seem to snap out of my routine. MBW was different after coming back from deployment, which is a big transition, and I knew the psychological part of returning home from war is not easy. We honestly needed help with our marriage, we started seeing a marriage counselor, and it helped a little bit, but the biggest thing that helped was the night I heard that bartenders voice.

"Brodee, Brodee, are you okay?".

Sometimes I tell myself, it wasn't so much about the drinking that I went to rehab, but it was also about the last thirty years of my life. There were happy moments. My son being born, marriage, vacations, but I felt I needed to hit the reset, I was done with one career and needed to put it behind me. I just couldn't figure out how to do it. After retirement from the military I had a lot of animosity towards some people, and I held on to it and couldn't let it go.

Thankfully, attending rehab helped me get out of that darkness I was feeling, and it brightened my world. I starting doing stuff in rehab I haven't done my whole life. I starting reading books, started meditating, my anger decreased, and best of all, for the first time since I can remember, I was remembering who I really was as a person.

I have told myself that I need to slowdown, and instead of surviving, I need to start living. I just want to breath, and not have the feeling of hatred, anxiety, or an unknown future, I just need to live for the day. Tomorrow is a new beginning.

This is how I went through the past forty. In my teens I never thought I would make it to eighteen, when I turned eighteen, I never thought I would make it to twenty one. At the age of twenty one, I never thought I would make it to thirty, I figured all my partying, drinking, and eating like shit would kill me. At the age of thirty, I told myself, there is no way I am making it to forty. My thirties was when my cholesterol was high, blood pressure borderline high, and anxiety was through the roof. Late thirties, I started telling myself, you better start watching what you eat, watch your stress level, and slow down on the partying. Then after all that worrying throughout the years, I made it to forty, and I want to continue to live, I want to live for a long time. I know death can happen at any time, but I am going to do everything I can do to live, I love breathing. That being said, I have stressed my whole life, and at the end of the day, I wasted time stressing, don't stress over living, everything always happens for a reason.

MIXTURE OF EVERYTHING

Its March 2019, I can't believe I have written a book, its taking me a little over a year, and it ended up being a lot of work. I am going to end with a few of my thoughts and opinions. Here we go:

Not sure about everyone else, but I sure am getting annoyed of the saying living the dream. When I ask someone how they are and they say that, I want to punch them. I feel that saying has become the most negative, sarcastic phrase and has worn out its welcome.

Here is what living the dream feels like. When my life is in order, and I have no stressors, I dream I am flying low over a green pasture, with small rolling hills, blue skies, shade trees scattered throughout my flight, and birds soaring above me. There is nothing more incredible than feeling yourself fly like Superman while sleeping, it feels so real. Another dream I recently had was the same dream every night for thirty days when I was in rehab. It was Rottweilers attacking me and killing a demon each night, so each morning I woke up I would be closer to mental stability. But there are bad dreams as well, the dreams of snakes, and running in place getting nowhere, dreams of drowning and other disastrous dreams. Sure enough when I have these dreams my life is chaos, something bad is usually happening at the present time.

There are people who actually are living their dream, maybe actors, professional athletes, doctors, pilots, etc...and good for them. A lot of people bash professional athletes, not me, I wish I would have taken the right path to play basketball. Athletes get paid, because the fans pay for the entertainment, so yes they do make millions, but they also have put in hours upon hours into becoming some of the greatest athletes on Earth. We don't know what it's like behind the scenes, but we as outsiders are quick to assume. Before you make assumptions about athletes not caring about the game, wear their shoes for a season and see if you can keep up with the busy life. It's the same with doctors and lawyers, I hear comments they get paid too much, well spend half your life in school and tell me they shouldn't get paid what they make. Now politicians on the other hand, those are overpaid crooks, complain more about what they make, because half of them are not worth a shit. While I am on the subject of athletes, I need to put something to rest, Michael Jordan is the G.O.A.T (Greatest Of All Time), Lebron James will never have the finesse Jordan had, matter of fact, Lebron James isn't even better than Kobe Bryant. There! It's said, and also to piss off my New England friends, Tom Brady is not the G.O.A.T., Joe Montana is the G.O.A.T.. Please don't burn my book☺

Unfortunately, we all know I never followed my childhood dream of being in the NBA, but I found a path, and gave it my all. Which I pushed myself to always work, I had a job since the age of fourteen. I am a true believer, if you work and continue to work, the American system will pay you back as you get older, some people disagree, but that's a whole other book titled "Entitlement".

One thing about this country is there are so many paths to take, for instance the path my brother took. He started working with Michaels Arts and Crafts as a teenager, he is now forty four, the district manager and making six figures. Then there is the college path, but know what you want to do before you jump degrees five times like I did, find your passion and study for it. Third, there is the trade school path, plumbers, farmers, electricians, mechanics, welders, you name it, they are respectable jobs and will always be needed. For real, technology is getting crazy, but humans still poo, regardless how high tech we are, so plumbers will always be needed. Then of course the athlete, singer and actor path, it takes a lot of talent to do what these people do, and we talk a lot of crap about them, but it's entertaining, and they are still human like me and you. Finally, the path that takes care of everyone above, first responders and the military. Nothing more valuable to our country then seeing men and women in police, fire fighting and military uniforms, they keep this country running, they are the back bone of our nation. But wait! I forgot one more group, the nurses, doctors, veterinarians, and veterinarian technicians that care for our wounded first responders and animals, we absolutely can't make it without their loving care.

All this makes me realize what an extraordinary world and nation we live in. Let's stop letting the 1% of bad people on this Earth bring 99% great people down.

Finally, remember your dream tonight. Either embrace that soothing dream of flying, or if it's a nightmare, look in the mirror in the morning and tell yourself, I will make changes to my life, until you are able to fly above those beautiful green pastures.

THIS IS THE END

The hardest part I encountered with writing a book is the end, it has taken me weeks to try to come up with the perfect conclusion, so I stopped thinking about it, and just waited until it popped in my head. It's weird, but I am sad I am done writing my book. Feels like for the past year I have been talking to someone about healing, as well as remembering my past, and I have no regrets. The best part is that the past makes us who we are in the present and the future, whether it be the wrong decisions you learn from, or great memories you cherish, keep living and pushing forward.

Before I finish, I have to thank people throughout my life that have help me become who I am as a human. Starting with my fourteen year old smarty pants son:

MAS: you have accomplished more than I ever did as a kid, you have also been through stressful times, your mom and I divorcing, me leaving with the military for long period of times, and you dealing with my anger sometimes, thank you for always understanding and being my son and best friend.

MBW: words cannot explain the love I have for you, no one has ever put up with me the way you do, we are strong together.

Maxwell: you and I have been through the gauntlet of life together, and for the past thirty years, no matter where we are in the world, I can always count on you.

Henry and Family: Henry, we have been through a lot together, and I know I always have your love unconditionally, I will forever be there for you, our families will grow old together, that's why God brought my family to Maine to be with you and your family.

Crack: you are the most laid back person I have ever known, and you know damn well you are my forever friend, I love meeting you at the bar on a Tuesday, or whatever day we decide and laughing while having beer. Here is Cracks quote, Keep the horse in the fight and the dog in the race, hahaha

DT: thanks for letting me be me, we were an awesome team when you were Platoon Sergeant and I was your right hand man, and thanks for always letting me vent to you about my final days in the military. You never judged me brother, you just listened, thanks DT.

LLF: Guten Tag, every six months for the past twenty years we talk, I look forward to it. I remembering when we met in Nuernberg Germany, I knew right away, we would be lifelong friends, I will always answer your call, I Love you Fuckkeee, and I love you F2. RIP brother!

H1: Sergeant First Class, you taught me how to be a great leader of Soldiers, I followed your example throughout my military career, great leaders like yourself are sadly a dying breed, you made me successful when I became a Platoon Sergeant. Soldiers First

Big pimpin: you are one of the funniest people I have ever met. I remember you were mimicking me in front of the platoon and I caught your ass making fun of me, hahaha, but I am an easy target. Keep making me laugh, I will call you before March Madness.

K Dawg: when I was down and out, you took me serious, I wasn't just a drunk, I wanted to end my life, and you took action to help me, I will never forget Kdawg, I love you.

KD: when I left to Germany I didn't have many friends, but I had you, I could always count on you to write me letters, I always looked forward to getting my mail overseas from you. There is nothing like writing letters, and receiving them in the mail, its priceless. I wish I kept all the letters we sent back and forth. But the big letter/package you sent me was when I was in Macedonia, you sent a Carton of Marlboros cigarettes and I loved you for that. I am blessed to still be talking to you this day, just know you helped me during my tour in Germany.

Brax: Brax doesn't know I exist, but he is a former classmate of mine from Smoky Hill High School, and he has Down Syndrome. Kids use to mock him and other disabled children at school, kids can be mean. I never did, I always had a huge heart for mentally challenged people. My biggest pet peeve in the world is when I hear the word retarded used as a derogatory term for something stupid a person did. I have even seen grown adults mock Down Syndrome people, and it pisses me off. Despite the ignorance from those 1% of people, Brax has worked at the local super market since high school. Every time I come back to Colorado, either from deployments, work trips or whatever, I always make a point to go to see Brax at the super market. Thanks Brax! you are my motivator when it comes to beating the odds

Last night I dreamed of dolphins swimming around me and I placed my hands on their sleek, smooth, rubbery body, it was breath taking. I woke up this morning and thanked God for all I had, and I always told my son and my Soldiers this. "If a person is in water and drowning, they should not panic and struggle so hard because eventually they will tire and drown, if they don't try hard enough and give effort they will slowly sink. Therefore, calmly tread water to stay afloat. I am at the point in my life where I am floating on my back in the open ocean with my eyes closed, and the warm sun penetrating my body, and floating along until I have to swim again.

"OOOHHHH SHHIIITTT!!!" My wife's water just broke, baby Moose is on his way. Time to start swimming again.